Happy To Be Me!

Learning to love who you are

By: Jerriann Savelle

1

Published by Jerriann Ministries
Granbury, TX.
www.jerriann.org
Printed in the U.S.A.

Scripture quotations are taken from the following:

ISBN 978-1-939934-03-1

Rights for publishing this book outside the U.S.A. or in non-English languages are administered by Jerriann Ministries, an international not-for-profit ministry. For additional information, please visit jerriann.org or, email jerriannministries@gmail.com, or write to Jerriann Ministries, PO Box 1354, Granbury, TX 76048, U.S.A.

This book is dedicated to . . .

Madison Elizabeth, my one and only daughter.

I'm so proud of the young lady you already are and how you always let

your light shine. I pray that daily, with your eyes fixed on Jesus, you will

grow more confident in yourself and realize how valuable you are.

There is only one you!

I hope that you learn from my hard lessons in life and they help prevent

you from going through the same sufferings.

I know you will be the woman God created you to be.

I love you!

ACKNOWLEDGEMENTS

I would like to say *thank you* to:

My six amazing children (Mark James, Preston, Madison, Dylan, Bryn, and Kai), who give me daily examples of my Father's love for me.

My godly parents, Jerry and Carolyn Savelle, for picking up the pieces of my life so many times. I honor the heritage of faith you have given me.

My precious grandmother, Mary Creech, for being my hero and everything I hope to be one day.

My "Ant" Shirley, who has always loved me unconditionally.

My awesome friend and editor, Michelle Bitner.

For all my loving friends that believed in me along the way.

And of course, more than anyone, my Lord and Savior, Jesus Christ; for giving His life for me and covering me in His love, His mercy, His grace and His peace. I am forever thankful.

Thank you!

CONTENTS

FOREWORD

I am happy for you today because you have a book in your hands that will change your heart, your mind, your life.

I've known Jerriann Savelle most of her life. She's been my Li'l Sis. Watching her these years I've seen her grow from a feisty, courageous little girl, to an innovative, passionate teen, to a determined young woman, and into the loving and devoted mother she is now.

As Jerriann faced difficulties and hurts in her life, it was painful for family and friends to watch. But we all knew this feisty, courageous, innovative, passionate, determined, devoted and loving woman had the Word and the Spirit of God in her. I had no doubt she would make it. And make it she did! And you can make it too!

That very courage, determination, and love allowed her to lay pride and privacy aside in order to reach you with the same love of God that reached her. Here she gives you the keys to the changes that made her life new. Jerriann's journey to the encompassing awareness of the love of Jesus will deepen your own awareness, no matter where you are at in your walk with Him.

I recommend *Happy To Be Me* to everyone! We have all struggled with these same feelings to one degree or another and we all know others who live with self-doubt and insecurity. This is one of those books that you will want to give away over and over again. This book will bring healing and wholeness to every person it touches.

Thank you Jerriann for your words of love and sweet surrender to the One who really loves us: our Lord Jesus. And for the record, I always thought you were sweet.

So reader, hear the message of this book and believe it.

Yes. Jesus does love me.

And Yes, He loves you too.

Open the book and see . . .

Kellie Copeland

INTRODUCTION

As far back as I can remember, I was an emotionally needy child. I know my mom and dad did the best they could to show me they loved me, but I needed so much more. I walked around with a cloud of sadness glooming over me, trying to cover it as best I could. I never felt good enough and really never liked myself. I assumed my parents' lives and those around me would be better off without me (heavy stuff for a little girl to carry around). I used to think, "I didn't ask to be born; I don't even want to be here." It's so very sad to think I lived for years with that mindset. It hurts my heart to think about it.

Early on, I was the troublemaker kid—the square peg who never fit in the round hole. I acted out for attention, somehow hoping to find my identity and finally like myself.

I only have one sister who is a year younger. She was always the good girl who never did anything wrong, unless of course, I persuaded her to do it. I grew up feeling like we had invisible labels: Terri the "good one" and Jerri the "difficult one." Since my label was there, I made sure I lived up to it! I was always in trouble with my parents and my teachers!

Instability and depression plagued me as a child. I was just never happy. My parents really didn't know what to do with me, except pray and speak God's Word over me.

As I ventured into my teen years, my search for value began to focus on the opposite sex. Boys had started to notice me, so I began to look to them for approval. I *always* had a boyfriend. Having a boyfriend and being in a relationship made me feel worth something and provided a fake sense of security. I felt special, if only for a time.

A cycle of endless relationships and heartbreak defined my teen years, which unfortunately continued on through my adulthood. It always began with the excitement of a new relationship and that buzz of "new love." Eventually it would lead to the pain of breaking up, which in turn led to an overwhelming need to replace the last boyfriend with a new one—a remedy for numbing the pain that only perpetuated the problem. It became my drug. I just could never get enough of that first feeling of new love (I use the word love loosely here).

In all of that, I still had no stability and true sense of who I really was. I was always looking for someone to give me the attention I needed. I failed to focus on what it was inside of me that needed so much attention, and fixing it. I was broken on the inside and needed healing and a changed heart. I was tired of being tired and desperate for change.

It took me a long time to stop the repeated events of broken relationships, to no longer be starved for attention from others, to learn how to be content within myself, and just be happy being me. After hitting a low point in my life and another divorce, I finally began to pull apart the layers of pain, the layers of rejection, the layers of longing to be accepted. What was revealed was the deep seated insecurity that had plagued me continually. I laid all of it at the altar of God and worked diligently to begin seeing myself through God's eyes of love and approval rather than through my own self-hate or the eyes of judgment and disproval of others. I have truly discovered just how much God loves *me*, and it's a beautiful thing.

This is my story, and maybe you can you identify with my life in some way.

Have you jumped from relationship to relationship, looking for the "perfect one" to make it all better?

Have you done things you later regretted, trying to fill the void or mask the pain?

Have you brought insecurities from your childhood into your adult life?

Do you still find yourself struggling for acceptance with others and especially yourself?

Do you fear if people knew the real you, they wouldn't like you?

Do you look in the mirror and feel disgust at the reflection staring back?

If you answer yes to any of the above, then my friend, I pray that the words written in this book reach gently into your heart and help set you on the path for change, so you can begin living the dream life God wants for you:

A life free from hang-ups, free from fear, free from defeated living.

You may have experienced moments of freedom in the past, but now realize, insecurity and low self esteem have crept back into your life and have taken up residence again. It's time to settle this once and for all—it's time to get free from the things that have been holding you back all your life! No more stopping and starting!

The freedom I'm talking about allows you to no longer be dependent on anyone else's opinion of you, but in the One who made you complete!

I have no great words of wisdom, but I know someone who does. I don't have it all figured out, and I don't get it right every time, but I know someone who does; His name is Jesus. I want to share with you what He has done for me.

He loves us; He had adopted us as His Children; we belong to Him. This makes us valid, worthwhile. We are truly significant in the eyes of God despite our human feelings or the comments of our critics.

Psalm 95 (Psalms Now)

CHAPTER 1

Desperate for Attention

Desperate:

Reckless or dangerous because of despair or urgency

Having an urgent need; desire

Extreme or excessive

Having no hope or giving into despair

I'm embarrassed to say, but *desperate* defines how I spent most of my teens, my 20s, and yeah, most of my 30s too. Just saying the word has a pathetic tone to it, doesn't it? Well, that defined me: desperate for validation and reckless in my pursuit for acceptance.

From the outside, I looked put-together. I even won several awards during my school years from "Class Favorite" to "Freshmen Princess." I had everything materially a girl could dream of and was able to travel to amazing places. Yet, none of that mattered because I was always searching for someone to give me that magical feeling that would take all the pain away, love me forever, and bring value to my life. In my mind, I lived in a soap opera fantasy world where I would meet the perfect boy and we would live happily ever after. My whole existence depended on looking for someone else to make me happy. I wanted to be Cinderella and find my Prince Charming. Sadly, that search led to years and years of pain and brokenness, not only hurting myself, but others along the way.

Never put the key to your happiness in

somebody else's pocket.

I can close my eyes now and picture myself as a teenager, sitting on my bed, crying my eyes out, and feeling like it was the end of the world because another boy had broken my heart. I would put my all into every relationship and end up with nothing. I never enjoyed life or lived in the moment because the drama of my current relationship consumed my every thought and action.

Boys don't like desperate girls. Boys like hard to get girls and confident girls. I was neither.

I tried so hard to act like I didn't care, but I would eventually go back to my desperate ways, trying to be everything they wanted me to be. If they liked soccer, I started liking soccer. If they liked country music, I tried to like country music, even though I can't stand it. (Sorry for you country music lovers.) My pathetic pursuit for acceptance never won at this ridiculous charade I called love. Every time I tried to become what someone else wanted, I just lost more of who I was. When a good guy would show up in my life, I didn't know how to value him and would usually dump him for a bad boy. I didn't have the confidence to value myself and believe I was worth something, much less another person's love.

Insecure people do not see themselves as valuable. Something that is valuable is to be cherished and protected and not easily given away. Insecure people are always giving out in hopes of getting something back. The giving away is not unconditional because the insecurity is always looking for something in return—acceptance, validation, love, approval, value, worth. Yet, it never comes.

You do not belong to yourself, for God bought you with a high price. So you must honor God with your body.
1 Corinthians 6:19-20 (NLT)

I remember a popular song when I was in Jr. High, sung by Johnny Lee. It was called, *Looking For Love In All The Wrong Places.* The title rings true for many girls willing to sell themselves short, looking for love. Because of their insecurity, they are easily charmed and enticed by the first guy who comes around telling them they are pretty. I was that girl.

Insecurity can be detected in people in many different ways. It's obvious to see in some people who are withdrawn; walking with their heads down, never making eye contact. Others may be harder to detect. They can be the life of the party by being loud, daring, bold, but really they are just acting out based on their insecurities. Desperate people do desperate things. Insecurity and having a lack of value can often lead some to promiscuity or alcohol and drugs to escape reality. Insecurity also causes some to isolate themselves, being considered a loner or socially awkward. It's destructive and unhealthy in any form.

I never thought of myself as a fearful person. I wasn't afraid of the dark, or spiders, or heights. Yet I never realized growing up that inferiority and feeling less than others, is also a form of fear . . .

• The fear of being rejected

• The fear of not being accepted

• The fear of never being good enough

Those types of fear were embedded deeply within my soul and grew more intense with each broken relationship. Joy and peace were gradually draining from my life.

In high school there was a pretty, outgoing cheerleader who had a lot of guys interested in her. Regardless, she was not "boy crazy" and was nonchalant toward guys. Even as a teenager, her attitude left an impression on me. She was not bothered by all of that attention, and I so wanted to be like her, but my insecurity wouldn't let me.

A good woman is hard to find, and worth
far more than diamonds.
Proverbs 31:10 (MSG)

I was raised in a Christian home, in fact my daddy is a preacher, so I heard the truths of the Bible all my life. I always loved Jesus and never once doubted He loved me. I prayed, read my Bible, and went to church every time the doors were open. I was taught right from wrong, but despite my spiritual upbringing, I chose to live by my feelings and emotions. Whatever felt good at the moment guided my way. I was up, or I was down, and I could change at a moment's notice. I had no stability, and insecurity completely controlled my life. I listened and accepted the lies the devil had put in my head at a very young age. I walked around wearing titles I had acknowledged as truth about myself:

"Failure"

"Rebel"

"Problem Child"

"Never Good Enough"

And the list went on and on.

I displayed my titles for all to see and acted accordingly.

Do you have imaginary titles hanging over you—titles that you've been carrying around for far too many years? Have you accepted them as truth?

When you live with a feeling of insecurity surrounding you, you can be told everyday you are special, but if you don't believe it, no one can convince you otherwise. It doesn't matter how many books you've read or how many church services you've attended looking for change, if you don't see yourself as valuable and believe you are worth something, you will never change. Change always has to take place on the inside first, in your heart.

Has insecurity robbed you of living a life of confidence and stability?

Do you have a hard time saying "no" to people based on your fear of rejection and your need for approval?

God never designed for you to be inferior or insecure in any area of your life! You should never feel inferior to anyone else. It is time for you to walk in the truth and know you are special, you are beautiful, and you are unique! There is only one you, and the world is a better place because you are in it! Don't go another day with the lie that you are less than anybody. You are just as good as anyone else, but you are the only one who can change yourself and the way you carry and see yourself. No one else can do it for you . . . just *you*! Are you ready for change?

More Drama

I had gone to a Christian school most of my life, but I convinced my parents my Sophomore year of high school to let me transfer to public school; and what a huge transition it was for me. This bigger exposure to peer pressure, added with the already longing need for acceptance, contributed greatly to much of the negativity that followed me and shaped whom I would later become in life. Being the new girl is never fun, but especially not at a rural school where almost everyone had grown up together. I was new bait for the guys, and the girls hated me right from the start. I was bullied on many occasions, from my locker being trashed, to my car tires being slashed. To be honest, it was hell.

I was struggling with insecurity already and desperately wanting to fit in, like most teenagers, so walking into this "shark fest" of jealous, mean girls certainly didn't help.

I can vividly recall one afternoon hearing the buzz circulating around the school that a group of girls were out to get me. The last bell rang at the end of the day, and as fast as I could, I ran to my car and sped out of the parking lot! I had escaped, but my quick sigh of relief quickly diminished when I looked in my rear view mirror to see I was being followed home by at least twenty other cars (I'm not exaggerating)! They surrounded our yard, most of them spectators to the ringleader's threats. I had broken rules, so they said, and I was to pay. My dad stepped in and cleared the scene while I laid on my bed and cried my eyes out. I felt like the loneliest girl in the world. This episode only damaged my sense of self-worth even more. I grew a tough shell on the outside, (I couldn't let them see me cry) while still bleeding for approval on the inside.

Fear and rejection became my closest companions.

Anger and defensiveness, my body guards.

Regardless of age, we all want to feel validated and accepted, but the teen years can be some of the toughest. Most teens struggle with insecurity and low self-esteem to some degree, making junior high and high school years brutal at times, feeling like you never measure up: aren't pretty enough, skinny enough, or cool enough. Then add bullying and harassment to the mix, and tragically for some, it's unbearable. Some even choose to end their life. I made it through high school with the help of my mom pushing me along, but I was literally counting the days down until graduation. Our alma mater said something like, "Hail to friendship, hail to loyalty" and I always sang it, "To hell with friendship, to hell with loyalty." I hated that place and hated what they had done to me.

I'll never forget another moment in high school that affected me in such a way that it left its mark for a very long time. I was on the drill team, and each week we had to audition in groups in front of the rest of the team to show we knew the routine and were ready to perform it at the game that week. I practiced every day, right along with the rest of the girls, and was confident at audition time that I knew it. I would get in my group and see this clique of mean girls looking and laughing, while pointing at me. I would get so nervous and caught up in what they thought about me that I would start messing up and forget some of the steps. Many times, I wasn't able to perform at that week's game with the rest of team and would have to sit on the sidelines because I didn't make the cut. It was so embarrassing and humiliating because I knew the routine, but I had let them defeat my confidence. Being laughed at and made fun of is never easy to deal with. Every incident just added another brick of insecurity and layer of pain around my heart. The walls were growing taller and thicker with each passing day. Hurt and offense were the bricks; insecurity was the mortar.

I wasn't strong enough inside to stand up to the challenges

that came from my high school years and suffered greatly because of it. It took years to undo.

> 66 NO ONE CAN MAKE YOU FEEL INFERIOR
> WITHOUT YOUR CONSENT. 99
> *ELEANOR ROOSEVELT*

Unfortunately, some of us take those negative experiences from our teen years into our adulthood and allow them to form us into the damaged people we become. Rather than moving forward from my hurtful experiences in high school and learning from them, I continued to carry them. My ever growing need for acceptance, my longing for validation, and a feeling of inadequacy only added more weight to the baggage already weighing me down.

Like me, you may have had moments that left their mark on you. Maybe you were laughed at and made fun of, and you've carried those painful memories around in your heart. You may even be oblivious to their impact, but they have probably contributed to the insecurity you've lugged around for years. Carrying around all the painful events from the past can get very heavy!

Is your load heavy now? Are you tired of carrying all of

those memories around with you?

> *Then Jesus said, Come to me, all of you who are weary*
> *and carry heavy burdens, and I will give you rest. Take*
> *my yoke upon you. Let me teach you, because I am*
> *humble and gentle at heart, and you will find rest for*
> *your souls. For my yoke is easy to bear, and the burden I*
> *give you is light.*
> Matthew 11:28-30 (NLT)

As I grew older, I just assumed people didn't like me, mainly girls. I could walk into a room full of girls and already have my mind made up, "They won't like me." I became "one of the boys" with a group that had become like brothers to me. I felt safer with them, rather than risk being rejected by friendships with girls. I fell right into the trap the devil had set for me every time. I was always being played, and he always won.

I clearly remember being at a football game one night, and these two girls kept staring at me to the point of making me uncomfortable. I actually started to get annoyed by their constant staring. I kept thinking, *What are you looking at? Stop staring at me!* They eventually walked up to me, and I felt my guard rising, ready to protect myself since I assumed they were coming to verbally attack me. One girl said, "I like your dress," and the other said, "You are so pretty." I was taken back at the compliments and embarrassed at the thought that I almost told them off for just looking at me. My confidence and self-image were depleted to the point of defensiveness. Insecurity controlled my life in every way.

I was quiet in certain settings, and some would mistake me for a snob. Other times, I showed off and was loud, trying to be cool. If ever dared to do something crazy and outrageous, I always rose to the challenge, subconsciously hoping it would bring acceptance. If only they could have seen the trembling little girl hiding inside my rebellious exterior, screaming "Please accept me!" The message was very clear in my troubled mind, "Girls hate me, and guys use and abuse me." (Isn't it interesting, but not a coincidence at all, that God's plan for my life has always involved a ministry focused on helping women. I have a heart for women and the issues they go through. That's just like Jesus though; He takes our painful experiences from the past and allows us to use them to help others become free.)

Insecurity is so crippling and so exhausting. We "appear" to have it all together while struggling on the inside. Fear of not being accepted for who we are paralyzes us and gives Satan a foothold. Insecurity causes people to continually try on different "masks" or ideas of what others may want them to be, hoping to find the right "look" that will meet the approval of others. It might begin in high school with the "Party Girl" mask that says, "I'm cool. I'm in with all this partying if you will accept me." The "Perfect Student" mask says, "If I make straight A's, my parents will be proud, and then they'll love me." There's also the "Tough Guy" mask worn by those who bully others in hopes of being respected by their peers, yet inside they feel weak. These masks are often carried right into our adult lives. How about the "Superwoman" mask that says, "I can do it all. I have it all together." Yet secretly cringing at the thought of the other soccer moms knowing we're falling apart or that our lives are not as perfect as they think, while wearing the "Perfect Marriage" mask. We desperately hold onto masks that keep things hidden, never wanting others to see face value—the real deal. Hiding behind a false idea or image of the real you is low self esteem hard at work, attacking your worth as an individual. Insecurity never allows you to be comfortable in your own skin, and keeps you from saying, "This is who I am, flaws and all, but I'm still okay with me."

Insecurity comes straight from the devil; he attempts to keep you stifled and fearful all your life, never letting you just be yourself.

> 66 ALWAYS BE A FIRST RATE VERSION OF YOURSELF AND NOT A SECOND RATE VERSION OF SOMEONE ELSE. 99
>
> *JUDY GARLAND*

I knew a precious woman who passed away several years ago. She always felt less than others and that she never measured up. Insecurity controlled her life. I remember sitting down and talking with her, while she vividly recalled the moment in her childhood that insecurity took over. It had left its ugly mark, and she never truly freed herself from it. It plagued her all of her life. She fearfully and timidly focused on what she lacked. She had amazing qualities, but never recognized them. Sadly, she never lived out her full potential.

Why settle with a life filled with inferiority?

Why live with fear?

Why continue to wear the mask?

A feeling of rejection always goes hand and hand with insecurity. The devil continuously set me up with opportunities to feel rejected. He knew my weaknesses, and I fell often for his tricks. This might sound dumb, but this happened to me often and still does on occasion. I can meet someone and have a conversation with them, but the next time I see them, they don't remember me at all. Only after I remind them of our previous meeting do they recall, saying, "Oh yeah, now I remember you," making me feel completely insignificant. I can't tell you how many times this has happened to me. I know it's not the person intentionally trying to make me feel insignificant, but I have finally realized it's just another one of the many strategies of the devil to make me feel inferior. It may be nothing to someone else, but when you battle with insignificance and insecurity, it becomes magnified. The devil will try *anything* to keep you feeling insecure and rejected, which inevitability brings defeated living. They are just Satan's little tests along my journey to see if I am really free.

Perhaps you've had some of these tests too:

Did someone ignore your comment on their Facebook page?

Did someone walk past you at work and not speak?

Did someone not return your call?

Did someone invite everyone to the cookout, except you?

If you have battled with insecurity, then you know exactly what I'm talking about. Becoming easily offended often partners with insecurity. When insecure, you can be overly sensitive, and little things hurt your feelings all the time. Insecure people seem to take everything personal, becoming defensive. They feel left out and overlooked. The littlest slight by someone becomes a huge offense. Insecure people are usually negative and assume the worst. They often have their guard up and their "offense radar" on with a big chip on their shoulders.

Have you laid in bed at night and internalized the offense of what "they" said and how "they" treated you? Did you get angry at yourself for letting it affect you so easily and for being so weak?

How do I know? Because I've done it.

I was hurt and defensive most all the time. Do I still have opportunities to feel this way? Of course I do, but now I recognize them as set ups from the devil, and don't fall for them like I did. Spending time in God's Word has better equipped me to handle them when they occur. I know who I am in Christ Jesus; therefore that makes me confident in who I am. My significance no longer comes from someone responding to my phone calls, liking my comments, or remembering me; I'm significant to Jesus, and I matter to Him!

You have to make yourself (hurt feelings and all) look beyond the hurtful situations and see them for what they are: a set up, a ploy, a plot, a scheme—all tactics from the devil! He is so malicious in his deception. Not only will he set you up, but then once you fall for the ploy, he will throw condemnation on you for falling for it in the first place! You then mentally beat yourself up for failing once again.

You're so pathetic!

You're so immature!

You're so stupid!

And once again the self-hate cycle begins.

Don't give into that! The devil knows your weak areas and tries to bring opportunities to trip you up. He will try his best to exclude you and make you feel like you don't matter. The devil wants you to dwell on a situation or scenario that hurts your feelings. He wants you to go over and over it in your mind until it consumes your thought life. If you are not careful, those thoughts of offense can lead to anger and bitterness, which he will use to defeat you.

> *Don't be too quick to get angry because anger lives*
> *in the fool's heart.*
> Ecclesiastes 7:9 (CEB)

Instead, you have to get to the place where you can laugh at the devil and his pathetic attempts to try to keep you down. The insecurity challenges and tempts you to react, but the more you are able to resist, the less frequently they will control you because you have resisted inferiority. In the past, a situation may have upset me for days, but now it may only affect me for hours or minutes or not at all. I can shake them off more quickly than before because I am not as sensitive, and feel secure in my position with Christ.

Keep in mind, often people have no idea they have hurt your feelings and would feel horrible if they knew they had. Other people are down right rude and nasty, hoping they hurt you. Regardless, you have to shake it off and keep moving—confident in being you because your Heavenly Father knows and loves you.

Throughout the years, I have read hundreds (yes, hundreds) of self-help books, trying to change and better myself. I hoped that in all the reading, I could figure out how to stop myself from continually making poor decisions due to my lack of confidence and self-worth. Although the books I read were inspiring, nothing ever lasted, and I eventually went back to my old self-defeating thinking and my old self-defeating ways. I had head knowledge of how to change and what to do, but my heart needed to change first.

Can you relate?

Do you know what you need to do but somehow never have a complete change on the inside? Do you continually revert back to your patterns and old ways of doing things?

Is insecurity and fear holding you back from having a successful life?

If so, then it sounds like you need a heart change, like I needed. You need a healing transformation to set you free and break the chains of insecurities, addictions, and hang-ups from your past.

Matters of the Heart

The condition of your heart determines the direction of your life. What is down in your heart will always be reflected in your thoughts, your attitude, and your actions. Your heart dictates your course. When you live a life of doing things on your own (living in your flesh and doing whatever feels good), your heart has become stubborn and prideful. God hears you saying, "I can do this on my own; I don't need You to show me the way." Proverbs 4:23 says, "Guard your heart above all else, for it determines the course of your life." The Amplified Bible says to be vigilant (careful and watchful) about protecting your heart. To guard your heart means to protect what's going in it.

Picture a soldier watching guard.

He is alert and attentive about what is going on around him. We have to be this way about our hearts. It's vital to be on guard because your heart determines the course of your life!

A hard heart is a heart that has closed the door to God's leading and guiding for one's life. Often times in an attempt to protect ourselves from more heartbreak and hurt, we can become stubborn and allow ourselves to become closed off from others. A hard heart leads to a tough way of life, but there is a better way.

When your heart aligns with God, you want to do everything you can to please Him. A pure heart desires to follow and obey the Lord and His direction. Your heart desires faithfulness and loyalty to God and His ways for your life, not your own. Following after God and keeping a pure heart will keep you from making mistakes, based on insecurities and fears.

I will take away your stubborn heart and give you a new heart and a desire to be faithful. You will have only pure thoughts, because I will put my Spirit in you and make you eager to obey my laws and teachings.
Ezekiel 36:26-27 (CEV)

I can think of so many times I just had to do it my way. I wanted instant results rather than waiting on God's direction for my life. Think of all the messes we can avoid in our lives, if we will just patiently and steadily follow after His ways rather than our own! Often times, we get in a hurry trying to make things happen for the "perfect" life, usually only resulting in disaster.

You have to completely surrender to Him, every part of you, and it begins with the heart. Surrendering requires completely giving up and abandoning your old ways of doing things. It cannot be just a half way thing; it must be a total surrender of your flesh wanting to have its way all the time. Your spirit, mind, will, emotions, and body must all be in tune with what God wants for your life. Ask yourself:

Has doing things my way gotten me where I really want to be in life?

Do I like the direction my life is headed right now?

Am I living the life I truly want?

Do I find myself wanting to do the right thing, but ending up always doing the wrong thing?

The time is now to raise the white flag and surrender your ways and become sensitive to God and His purpose for your life. His way far surpasses anything you could come up with—without the pain and heartache we often get ourselves involved in. Our flesh wars constantly with our spirit. It always wants to be boss and dictate our actions.

So, I say let the Holy Spirit guide your lives. Then you won't be doing what your sinful nature craves. The sinful nature wants to do evil, which is just opposite of what the Spirit wants. And the Spirit gives us desires that are opposite of what the sinful nature desires. These two forces are constantly fighting each other.

Galatians 5:16-17 (NLT)

Our sinful nature never produces anything good and lasting in our lives. It always wants to do what feels good at the moment; without consideration of the long-term consequences. Oh, the sin might be enticing and fun for a time, but the temporary high always ends in heartache, pain, and loss. I just saw on TV this week a young actor who was found dead from a drug overdose, who was supposedly living the good life. Temporary highs never give permanent happiness. Daily we must nail our hang-ups and fleshy desires to the cross—those things that constantly hound us (you know yours well). They have to be brought *daily* to the Lord so that your flesh doesn't try to take control because it will if not dealt with. It all comes down to the condition of the heart. We can't fix things in our lives with our old heart in control. Let that old way of doing things die, just like Jesus died on the cross for all your sins.

That is why it's so important to wash our hearts daily, just as we do our physical bodies. Pray Psalm 51:10 every morning over yourself:

"Create in me a clean (pure) heart, O God; and renew a right (loyal, steadfast) spirit within me."

Having a pure heart and living a life that pleases God leads to a lifetime of contentment and peace, instead of constantly living with messes you have created in a feeble attempt to find your own kind of contentment. There is no better way to live than with a pure heart and a steadfast spirit that's connected to your Heavenly Father.

Choices

We make hundreds of choices throughout the day, from small ones (what you will wear, or what you will eat) to big ones (where you will live, what occupation you will have, or who you will marry). Daily decisions present themselves and can be critical in steering your life in the direction in which it will go. One wrong choice can change your life forever. Think of a choice you've made that dramatically changed your life. Most of us have experienced life altering events due to a choice made. Someone could be in a hurry to get married and just settle by marrying the wrong person. Someone else could decide to get behind the wheel after a night of partying, and that one choice can change their life instantly. Every choice has a natural or spiritual end result that is either good or bad.

Our lives are a reflection of the choices we have made.

What about our heart choices? There are consequences to...

Choosing to stay angry.

Choosing to stay inferior.

Choosing to stay bound.

I always wanted to do right, but usually ended up doing wrong because I lived by my flesh most of the time. Living by the flesh is your sin nature, being controlled by feelings and emotions at the moment. I love how the Apostle Paul explains his struggle to choose between doing right and doing wrong. He says, "I don't really understand myself, for I want to do what is right, but I don't do it. Instead, I do what I hate. So I am not the one doing wrong; it is sin living in me that does it. And I know that nothing good lives in me, that is, in my sinful nature. I want to do what is right, but I can't. I want to do what is good, but I don't. I don't want to do what is wrong, but I do it anyway. But if I do what I don't want to do, I am not really the one doing wrong; it is sin living in me that does it. I have discovered this principle of life—that when I want to do what is right, I inevitably do what is wrong. I love God's law with all my heart. But there is another power within me that is at war with my mind. This power makes me a slave to the sin that is still within me. Oh, what a miserable person I am! Who will free me from this life that is dominated by sin and death? Thank God! **The answer is in Jesus Christ our Lord**" (Romans 7:14-25 NLT).

Sound familiar? He amazingly sounds like most of us in the constant struggle against our flesh. Most of us want to do what is right, but we usually end up doing the wrong thing because our flesh has been in control for so long. Our natural reaction screams to go with the flow of our flesh, letting our emotions and feelings dictate the actions we take and the decisions we make.

Flesh always wants instant gratification. It never stops to think of the repercussions to come. Think about the following scenarios:

You want to stay sober, but decide to go out with friends who drink because, after all, that one drink won't hurt.

You sleep with that guy, even though you know it's degrading and based on lust.

You max out your credit card *again* because you "just had to have it!"

You need to lose weight, but eat that second piece of cake and justify it because there are worse things!

All of these are choices of the flesh. I have learned the hard way that you will always pay for making a choice in your flesh. Immediate and temporary gratification coupled with impulsive behavior never brings lasting fulfillment.

Lately, I've struggled with my flesh where eating is concerned. I love carbs and sweets! All of my life, I have been small and never concerned with my weight. In my twenties, if I felt I was gaining a little extra, I could just skip a meal, and I would be right back where I was. It doesn't work that way in my forties, and wow, have I gotten a rude awakening! I can't eat whatever I want anymore. I used to be able to eat cakes, donuts, breads, or whatever I was craving with no problem, but not now. My flesh tries to lie to me, telling me, "It's ok, you don't eat that badly; one donut won't hurt." Somehow my flesh forgets to remind me that I already had one (or maybe two)! I can be looking online for new meal ideas to make for my family and catch myself looking at all the yummy desserts instead! It all comes down to choices: will I cave into what my flesh wants, or will I be disciplined where my diet is concerned?

Over-eating, blowing up in anger, sleeping around, spending too much money, partying, jealously, worrying—these are all choices.

Every day in some form or another, I can promise you, you will struggle with your flesh wanting to be in control. It's like a small child stomping to have its own way all the time! You have to get tough on your flesh and take back control, instead of being controlled! The Apostle Paul said, "I discipline my body like an athlete, training it to do what it should" (1 Corinthians 9:17 NLT). The only way to win this flesh battle is "in Jesus." Only Jesus can change and resolve that inner struggle. You've proven you can't do it on your own. By putting Him first in everything you do, your fleshy nature will die. When your flesh dies, then all those sins your nature craves will no longer rule and reign in your life. Fighting your flesh is an ongoing battle, but the more you practice making right choices, the more you will begin to see positive changes occurring in your life.

Making right choices is vital.

Most of the bad events that happened in my life resulted directly from poor decisions I made. I couldn't keep blaming "this experience" or "that person," making myself a powerless victim. I had to stop throwing pity parties because I thought life wasn't fair. Instead, I had to look right in the mirror and accept that the girl staring back at me was responsible for the choices I had made. No one had made me do anything. Like it or not, I was a sum total of every choice I had ever made.

Sitting where you are right now, your life represents all the decisions you have made up to this point. Depressing to think about? You know you can't keep living the way you have been; making the same wrong decisions, yet expecting something different to come out of it. If you want different results in your life, then you have to begin making different choices. It's that simple! It begins with one good choice at a time. You may be thinking, "I want to do the right thing, but this has controlled me all of my life, and I keep messing up."

Change begins with:

One step, one good choice.

Another step, another good choice.

The steps of a good man are ordered by the Lord.
Psalm 37:23 (NKJV)

Wouldn't it be wonderful if God would snap His fingers and miraculously make our lives exactly the way we want them? We all know it doesn't work that way. He has the best plan and the best way for you to follow, better than you can ever imagine, but again, *you* have to make the choice to get there.

In Deuteronomy 30:19 God says, "Today I have given you the choice between life and death, between blessings and curses

. . . Oh, that you would choose life . . ." (NLT).

I love that God gives us advice at the end of this scripture, "Oh, that you would choose life . . . " I know as a parent, I so want my kids to make good choices and avoid having to experience the pain, heartbreak, and setbacks that come from bad choices. Any good parent feels that way. I might explain to them why making that decision would be wrong, but ultimately they have to make their own choices. Your Heavenly Father feels the same way about you. He doesn't want you to go through failure and pain because of wrong choices. He's saying to you right now, "Choose life! Choose My way for your life." He can't make you choose anything, but He desires for you to choose the good life!

There is life in good choices and death in bad ones. Life choices are always moving you forward, while death choices are always taking you backwards. Making the right choices for your life can take you from always being the victim to the victor!

Don't be overwhelmed and self-defeated by thinking, "I never get it right." Instead, start getting it right today! If you mess up and make a wrong choice, repent, pick yourself up, and keep going! We get conditioned to being the way we've always been, living with the bad choices we have made, but your next choice can be the right choice.

When an opportunity comes your way to do something the

way you've always done it (the wrong way), stop and think, "Is this a life choice or a death choice?" If you are always quick to give someone a piece of your mind when you're really mad; wait, stop, and think, "Will this decision produce good things in my life, or will it produce negative outcomes?" You can never take back words that were spoken in anger, what's your choice going to be?

Yes, we serve a God that can restore our lives when we've made the mistake of submitting to what our flesh wanted, but why make God clean up your mess (again)? How much more time will you waste making the same wrong choices? He has good plans and a good future waiting for you, but it's up to you to get there by making right choices and seeing those good plans and a good future come to fruition in your life. Making the choice to follow after God and His plan for your life doesn't ever hurt you or bring havoc to your life. Why would we ever choose any other way? But again, it's *your* choice. He gives you free will. He can't make you do anything.

Your life is your story and represents your choices. You want your life to reflect the good choices you have made. Making good choices (God choices) is just a decision away!

66 THE DECISIONS THAT WE MAKE TODAY WILL DETERMINE THE STORIES WE TELL TOMORROW. 99
CRAIG GROESCHEL

Habits

I'm not sure who to give credit for this saying, but I remember hearing it for the first time when I attended Bible school and thought it was powerful:

> Your thoughts create your words,
> Your words create your actions,
> Your actions create your habits,
> Your habits create your lifestyle,
> Your lifestyle creates your destiny.

Every action (choice) we make and routinely make (good or bad) becomes a habit, and all those habits turn into the lifestyle we have created. Your character has been developed through your habits and is daily expressed in your choices. You might be looking at your current condition and thinking, "Ugh! I don't like what I've created!" Then change it! Anybody can change if they make the determination to begin making positive choices. It doesn't matter how old you are—old dogs *can* learn new tricks! As I said earlier, change begins with one simple choice at a time. When you begin making godly choices and continue making them, you begin developing good habits in your life. This goes for any area of your life from relationships, to eating right, to your finances. Routinely good choices make good habits!

> " SUCCESSFUL PEOPLE ARE SIMPLY THOSE WITH
> SUCCESSFUL HABITS. "
>
> *BRIAN TRACY*

Take exercise for an example. We all want to be in shape, feel good, and look good too, but it takes consistency to make a habit of exercising. Every day we must make a choice to exercise to cause it to become a habit. Going to the gym or going for a walk two or three times a month does not make a habit. I have laughed at myself and my weak rationalization as to why I haven't been going to the gym. I've thought to myself, "If I'm not going to be consistent in going, then I might as well not go at all." But you should make the choice to go today, and then you make the same choice again tomorrow. Don't set yourself up for failure with excuses.

Your daily routines define your habits. You have to incorporate exercise into your routine to cause it to become a habit. Just like brushing our teeth isn't an option, nor should taking care of our bodies with exercise. God wants us to make good choices spiritually, financially, and physically.

So, how do you make a habit out of exercising? You start by putting your workout clothes and shoes out, you set a designated time, and you don't let anything interfere with that time for yourself. You have to prepare for success. You'll never start making good choices that become good habits if you don't ever do anything differently.

Want to have good habits with your money? Again, it goes back to those choices you make on a daily basis. Are you spending more than you make? Are you charging things on a credit card you don't really need? Do you have nothing in your savings account? If you are tired of living paycheck to paycheck, then you must sit down and take the time to create a plan and budget for getting out of that situation. You have to begin making decisive choices to get yourself out of the financial mess you've created. God's plan for your life doesn't involve being in debt, but you get to choose how and on what you spend your money. Do you have a habit of treating yourself to a $5 coffee every morning, and then coming up short on paying bills every month? Maybe that's a habit you need to break, so that $5 a day can be saved for bills. You can never go wrong establishing good money practices.

> ❝ WE BECOME WHAT WE REPEATEDLY DO. ❞
> *STEVEN COVEY*

Good habits are essential and vital in your walk with God. You will never have a deep and meaningful relationship with Him if you don't have the habit of spending time in His Word.

It should be part of your everyday life. What you heard on Sunday morning at church is not enough to keep you spiritually fed for the entire week, just as eating food once a week will never nourish you. You have to spend time in God's Word *daily* to keep you built up and strong. It's a guide and road map for your life. Open up your Bible and find a scripture you can think on, and say it to yourself throughout the day. There is life and power in His Word, but you have to open it first to find it, or it becomes just another book collecting dust on your bookshelf. For example, the scripture I found this morning in my daily reading was from Psalm 68:19 (KJV), "Blessed be the Lord, who daily loadeth us (ME) with benefits," which is a promise from God's Word that I'm speaking over my family. Getting in His Word and knowing His promises are necessary for living a peaceful life, and it has to become a habit. It can't be a once in a while thing, or only during desperate times that you decide to turn to God. Everyday, it must be a priority—whether things are going good or going bad; whether you're too busy or not. Everyday!

It's a habit you have to create through your daily choices. You have to set aside time to do this, or you will get too busy and never find the time (just like exercising). Have you ever noticed, we always find time for the things we love to do, but when it comes time to do those things important for successful living, somehow we just can't find the time. You know why?

Because it takes discipline, and discipline is a word none of us like. It involves work, effort, and going beyond the norm. If you have to set your alarm to remind yourself to spend time with God, then that's what you do until it becomes a habitual part of your every day life. I've discovered in my own life if I haphazardly go through my day with no plan, I'm just existing with no good habits established. I might start off with good intentions of things I want to accomplish, but if I don't have a plan for success, I usually get distracted, venturing off from the good thing I intended to accomplish. I'm naturally not a disciplined person and tend to be more spontaneous in my decision making. So, to cultivate discipline and become more productive, I have to have a daily list that I can check routinely. By doing this regularly, I have been able to create good habits; especially with my spiritual development. With a house as busy as mine (five kids at home and three dogs), I have to make myself stop everything and spend alone time with God, or something will always try to get in the way.

Consistency is the key for creating good habits.

Reading God's Word is not the only spiritual habit we must establish; prayer time is vital as well. I've discovered in my life there are different times of prayer, all significant for creating faith and staying in fellowship with God. There are prayers said first thing in the morning, before checking your "newsfeed" or email (I'm guilty of that). You are simply giving your day to God and thanking Him for all the good things in your life. This kind of prayer doesn't have to be hours and hours; instead it can be 15 minutes at the beginning of your day to start your day off right. Another type of praying is staying in an "attitude of prayer" throughout your day. This just means speaking heart to heart with Him all day long. I might be drying my hair, cooking dinner, folding clothes, or driving in my car; rather than thinking about random things, I just talk to Him like I would a friend (He should be your closest friend). Sometimes it may not even be out loud; instead it's a silent connection with my Heavenly Father, my thoughts focused on Him. Then there is the prayer time where I give my undivided attention; I'm doing nothing else but surrendering my spirit, soul, and body to God. This is referred to as being in your "prayer closet," completely alone with absolutely no interruptions or distractions (Matthew 6:6). When you are desperate for change in your life then you will commit yourself to going beyond rehearsed and recited traditional prayers. Cultivate a strong prayer life.

Prayer is a powerful tool we have been given to build our faith, strengthen our resolve, and quiet the raging storm in our minds. Prayer is essential for successful living and should never be taken lightly or for granted.

> " PRAYER MUST BE HABITUAL,
> BUT MUCH MORE THAN A HABIT. "
>
> *E.M. BOUNDS*

It is never too late to create good habits in your life. Always remember, your daily choices in every area of your life become your daily habits, so make good ones!

CHAPTER 2

What's Next?

My mom married my dad at 17 (and remains happily married), so I just followed in her footsteps and got married very young too (three weeks from my twentieth birthday). I had no real aspirations in life except to go to Hollywood and make it big (which I knew wouldn't happen) or get married and have babies so I did the latter. Unfortunately, my marriage didn't work out the same as my parents. Totally unprepared for marriage, I was selfish, immature, and still trying to figure myself out. I tried my best to play house, but I lacked the maturity to be a wife. I remained an insecure child inside, still needing to find myself. That marriage ended in divorce. I feel grateful for the children God blessed me with from it, and I have no regrets because of them. I do, however, regret that I carried all that baggage with me into my next marriage. I had been a single mother for 5 years and had many spiritual experiences and encounters with God during those years, but I still continued to search for "a man" to make it all better and "fix" me from the last relationship. Expecting someone else to be a savior never works. No person can meet all your needs. They are human and will fall short. I was still not able to love and be the "help meet" for my spouse that God talks about in Genesis 2:18. Expressing love to another person was extremely difficult when I didn't love myself.

I was rarely happy, never feeling settled on the inside. I drifted from one event to another in my life, looking for fulfillment. I lived in a "What's next?" state of mind. My life remained in a constant whirlwind of chaos. I would get married, get pregnant, move to another state, get divorced, start a job, end a job, and start dating again. It was crisis living at its worst. I had no contentment and no peace. Looking for the ultimate fulfillment, I continually searched for some great utopia, but it never came. My life had become a series of constant dramas, all because of my choices and selfish motives. I lived in state of frustration and mental anxiety, while desperately grasping to keep it all together on the outside. Are you exhausted reading this? I certainly was, living it!

I often wondered, *When will I ever be happy?*

I battled with depression and insomnia for years. One night the hopeless feeling of all my inadequacies came crashing down on me, and I tried to kill myself. I took an entire bottle of sleeping pills in hopes that I would never wake up. I was convinced no one would care anyway. Thankfully the sleeping pills had the opposite effect on me and kept me up all night instead. I was crying out for help. I would regroup enough to "appear" to be okay, but I lived with episodes of depression for years. I never attempted to take my life again, but I often entertained the thought of dying. I had enough sense to realize I didn't want to risk it and spend an eternity in hell. Oh, how I hate the devil. He will stop at nothing to try and beat down a precious child of God.

Year after year, I continued repeating the same stupid mistakes. The pattern remained the same. I wanted things to be different in my life, but it all went back to the condition of *my* heart and *my* choices. I needed a spiritual heart transplant. Meanwhile, Jesus patiently waited for me look to Him as my "fix all" and Savior, not just in word only, but in my actions and my everyday living. It was one thing to say He was my Lord; it was another to actually let Him be Lord of my life.

When I became rebellious and struck out on my own,
He waited patiently for me to return.
When I fell on my face in weakness and failure,
He gently set me on my feet again.
Psalm 105 (Psalms Now)

It reminds me of the story in the Bible of the Israelite children in the wilderness. They finally gained freedom and traveled from Egypt to Israel, the Promised Land. This trip should have only taken around 11 days, but they were constantly grumbling and complaining. They had no faith in God and what He could do. Here's what God said about them, "But my people would not listen to me. They kept doing whatever they wanted, following the stubborn desires of their evil hearts. They went backward instead of forward" (Jeremiah 7:24 NLT).

So a trip that should have taken around 11 days, instead took 40 years! Sounds crazy doesn't it? You might not want to think about it, but how many years have you wasted going around the same mountains in your life? You may have been like me, making the same bad choices over and over and over and over. You circle around and around, and yet wonder, "Why does this always happen to me?" It comes down to your heart and your choices. It always comes back to those two things: following after God and His will for your life, or following after the flesh.

Why spend another day, another month, or another year making the same decisions and expecting something different to come out of it? God wants us free from addictive cycles today and free from searching for "something" outside of Him to make it all better. He has been waiting for us to give up the fight and rely on Him. He is the ultimate fulfillment.

Trust in the Lord with all thine heart; and lean not unto thine own understanding. In all thy ways acknowledge him, and he shall direct thy paths.
Proverbs 3:5-6 (KJV)

Aren't you ready for peace? Isn't it time to stop the madness and get off the crazy train, finally letting Jesus become the conductor of your ways?

Feelings and Emotions

My happiness used to always be based on "the happenings" and immediate circumstances in my life. Whatever was going on at that very moment was the way I lived. My feelings and emotions dictated my life. If everything was going great, then I felt great; if things were going badly, then my feelings would control the rest of the day. It was emotional roller coaster living at its worst, going up and down all the time!

Feelings are so fickle and cannot be trusted. One day you may not "feel" like being married or you may "feel" like a failure, but you can't live by your feelings. Our feelings and emotions are unpredictable from day to day. There are times I am very confident in what God has called me to do, ready to tackle my day and accomplish great things. Then suddenly, my feelings and emotions can step in and change everything, based on something I heard or saw, an obvious stumbling block Satan manipulated for my fall.

Feelings and emotions are moody. You may get hurt by someone, and then all the sudden, you're being controlled by what "they" said and therefore being controlled by your feelings. Don't get me wrong, God gave us feelings and emotions; they can be a good thing. If we did not have them, we would be walking around like robots, but it's not wise or healthy to be controlled by them. Your feelings and emotions don't always represent the truth of a situation.

Fear is just an emotion and can be replaced with peace.

Doubt is just a feeling and can be replaced with assurance.

Insecurity is just an emotion and can be replaced with confidence.

Sadness is just a feeling and can be replaced with joy.

Life can just be down right hard and unfair at times. Things can be done and said that are so very hurtful. Right this moment, you may be hurting emotionally. You may feel like you've been kicked in the stomach and had the life knocked out of you. I know that kind of pain, and I'm certainly not making light of what you may be experiencing. Feelings are a real thing, but I want you to get to a place in your life where you are no longer dominated by your feelings and what has happened to you in the past (or what may happen to you in the future). This way of living is draining, causing you to stay emotionally exhausted all the time.

Jesus has offered us so much more in life than living with just the 'ups and downs' of our feelings. We can have joy in life that doesn't depend on the happenings. This joy can live on the inside of you whether everything is going right or going wrong on the outside. I have been through challenging times in recent years, and in the past when I solely lived by my emotions, these times would have crippled me emotionally, causing me to crawl into my bed and hide under the covers because I felt like my whole world had just collapsed at that moment. I don't live like that anymore. I sometimes feel like nothing is going right in my life, but I hold tightly to the joy on the inside of me. It can't be taken away just because of what's going on around me. This type of joy says, "Somehow, someway God will work this out for me." That kind of joy brings an inner peace that all is well, regardless of my present circumstances. Just yesterday, I was given some upsetting news; I felt frustration and worry immediately trying to seep in. I took a minute to cry, but I decided not to let it ruin my day. If I really believe God is going to work this situation out for me, then I have to act like I believe it. I chose to go play with my family rather than choosing to be ruled by my emotions. I didn't sit around and feel sorry for myself, and I didn't allow my feelings to rule my day, or my life, for that matter. Again, it starts with one godly choice at a time.

It's inevitable; life will bring challenges, pain, heartache, and opposition, but God has a remedy that can ease the load while going through the trial. He can give you joy that can carry you through, even in the darkest times, when you learn to tap into it. Remember that popular song *Don't Worry Be Happy*? That's exactly what God encourages, "Don't worry; I've got this! Be happy." Put a smile on your face; everything is going to be okay because God is working behind the scenes for you.

Growing up, I heard this phrase preached plenty of times:

"I'm not moved by what I see I'm not moved by what I feel, I'm only moved by what I believe, and I believe the Word of God."

Smith Wigglesworth

If only I had truly accepted in my heart and lived by it rather than just reciting it.

Don't carry the load of what you're going through around on your face or in your words. Instead, let His joy fill your heart, especially in the hard times. I've been through some very difficult situations at times that my friends never even knew about and would have been very surprised to find out.

I didn't talk about it; I just smiled on the outside and let that inner peace and joy from God work on the inside. That's not being fake; that's complete faith and trust in God to take care of you. True faith is confidence in His Word and in His ability to provide for you. It takes a spiritually strong person not to become weakened by the pitfalls of life, but instead to rise above current situations because Christ dwells on the inside of you, giving you a joy that only He can give!

> *And be not grieved and depressed, for the joy of the Lord*
> *is your strength and stronghold.*
> Nehemiah 8:10 (AMP)

Living with the "What's next?" mentality will always cause you to live unfulfilled and unsettled, but having the joy of the Lord creates contentment on the inside, regardless of the circumstances. Contentment allows you to enjoy *this* day, rather than constantly looking for something better down the road.

Embrace today and live for now, not when:

you get the right guy,
or the perfect job,
or the dream house,

or the new baby,

or the "I'm sorry."

Live now, and enjoy the journey!

Based on my experience (and this coming from someone who was called moody most of my life), the *only* way I know how to overcome living by emotions and fickle feelings (doubt, fear, depression, anxiety, anger, the list goes on and on) is by getting into God's Word. It's the only way I can get my mind off the circumstances around me, preventing me from slipping into, "How do I fix this on my own" mode or feeling sorry for myself. When I feel my emotions attempting to take over, I take a deep breath, calm myself down, and pray or pull out my Bible.

Recently we put our house up for sale and had a buyer within two days of putting it on the market. The interested buyers put earnest money down and had the inspection completed on the house. Things were moving quickly, so I began packing right away. Then one morning, I got a call from the realtor, and just as quickly as they had put an offer in, they backed out. Immediately, my emotions went from elation and anticipation, to deflation and disappointment. I had to dive into the Word before my emotions and feelings invaded my thoughts and my actions.

If we allow it to, we will be ruled by our emotions all day long. We'll be up in good times and down in the bad. It's mentally draining and depletes you of knowing real joy. Yet, most people choose to live that way.

When I am going through something and my emotions want to control me, many times I have opened up the book of Psalms and began reading and instantly a calm comes over me. (I have a book called *Psalms Now* written by Leslie F. Brandt. It is an excellent translation of the Psalms and one of my favorites.) I always find a passage in the Bible that relates exactly to what I am going through at that moment. God's Word becomes a calm in the storm. It's just like in Mark 4:39 when Jesus spoke to an actual storm and said, "Peace, be still." You can say the same thing to your mind, your will, and your emotions: "Peace, be still."

It goes on to say, "And there was [immediately] a great calm (a perfect peacefulness)" (AMP). There is no greater peace that exists than the peace that Jesus provides, even in the biggest storms of life.

Our Lord, you are the one who gives me strength and
protects me like a fortress when I am in trouble.
Jeremiah 16:19 (CEV)

After so much trial and error, I have finally realized I can't figure it all out on my own. I can't fix it all, and I can't always make it better. My answers have to come from God and His Word.

You might be thinking, "Ugh, the Bible is so difficult to understand and so boring. I get nothing out of it." Like you, there have been times in my life when the last thing I wanted to do was open my Bible. It seemed so dry, and I thought, "I've already read all those scriptures a hundred times before." If those same thoughts come to you, consider it just another opportunity (choice) to push those feelings down and find your peace. Opening your Bible with a heart hungry for change and desperate for answers will change your life!

I promise you, the Word of God will come alive in you. You will find something to relate to, and a little flicker of light will come on, and hope will begin to glow inside of you. The more you dig in and find scriptures that relate to you, the more excited you will become at finding the relevance God's Word has for your life!

How can you not experience peace and a calm coming over you when you read:

"Give your burdens to the Lord. He will carry them. He will not permit the godly to slip or fall" (Psalm 55:22 TLB).

"When my heart is faint and overwhelmed, lead me to the mighty, towering Rock of safety" (Psalm 61:2 TLB).

"Lord, when doubts fill my mind, when my heart is in turmoil, quiet me and give me renewed hope and cheer" (Psalm 94:19 TLB).

"He forgives all my sins. He heals me. He ransoms me from hell. He surrounds me with loving kindness and tender mercies. He fills my life with good things!" (Psalm 103:3-5 TLB)

In your excitement of finding scriptures relating to your suffering, your faith will build up, and you will find yourself no longer living off your feelings and emotions. The very thing you have been struggling with will suddenly become small in your thinking. It will no longer dominate your thoughts, emotions, and feelings, but the Word will stir you to life—life abundantly!

Only then will you live without worry about tomorrow.

Only then will you live in your faith for this day!

I encourage you not to stop reading the Word when everything seems better in your life and things are going just the way you want them. Often times we only go to God when we need His help, but we forget about Him and spending time in His Word when all is well. You can't let your defense down.

The Word of God is like medicine. If your doctor recommends you take a certain medicine for 30 days but you decide to stop taking it at day 15 because you've started feeling better, you will not get the full benefit of what the medicine was intended to do. You may "think" you've recovered, but the infection or illness may not be completely healed in your body. You have to continue taking your prescription for the duration. The same holds true with the Word; you can't stop reading His Word when you feel better. It's the best preventive medicine for any ailment or condition in life.

Make God's Word a daily part of your life because your feelings and emotions will take every opportunity they can to be boss and rule out what God says. Stop letting that happen! You can't allow yourself to live any longer with the ups and downs of life. Live in that joy that only comes from spending time in God's Word and finding out what He says the final outcome will be.

Change Your Thoughts

Every decision you make, and every action you take begins first in your mind with a thought. It's been said that we have between 12,000-60,000 thoughts per day. Whatever the amount, it's overwhelming! Some reports claim that 70-80% of those thoughts are negative and toxic. So, needless to say, your thought life has power! I'm sure you've heard that saying, "What you think, you become." Dwell on a thought long enough, and your actions will eventually veer in that direction.

Whatever your most dominate thoughts have been, they have played a major role in determining where you are right now in life. Fear, insecurity, and shame all begin with thoughts. If you don't feel like you're good enough to have something (happy marriage, nice house, stability, successful career), then most likely you won't. Your life has been and continues to be shaped by your thoughts. Your thought life and your heart are connected. Whatever is on the inside will always come out on the outside.

For a man's heart determines his speech.
Matthew 12:34 (TLB)

Growing up, I was a negative person and often pessimistic. I described myself as a deep thinker; when in actuality, I thrived on rehashing the lies put in my head by the devil. I readily accepted them as the truth. I still have opportunities to go "there" with negative thoughts, doubt, and fear. My human nature wants to automatically think on what could have been or what if or why or what they said, and so on, but it takes me, once again, getting back in my Bible, disciplining my mind to meditate on good things. It has everything to do with what I chose for my thought life. I can always tell when my thought life is not lining up with what God says and I've slacked off spending time in the Word because it always comes out my mouth. I will begin to worry and wonder about things until eventually my mouth will start speaking it. I have to remind myself, "That's not how I think or who I am anymore."

Let God transform you into a new person by changing the way you think.

Romans 12:2 (NLT)

We all have those opportunities to think on the negative and allow worry, fear, and our past to control our thoughts. The only way to change your mind, which in turn changes your thoughts, goes back to getting in God's Word and finding out what He says. Mind over matter and positive thinking are impostors for trying to make changes in one's life. God's Word is the **only** real way for change—permanent change. When you get in the Bible and find out the real truth, it begins to renew your mind and your thinking, and a transformation will begin happening on the inside of you. To transform is to dramatically change, to reform, to convert, to alter. Allow God's Word to change the damaged thinking you've accepted until now. When you begin to think differently, you will begin to act differently.

**You will never be able to change your actions
if you can't control your thoughts.**

Your old way of thinking will always try to creep back in if
you allow it. Your momma may have said to you growing up,
"If you can't say anything nice, don't say it at all." You have to be
the same way with your thought life; if you can't think anything
good, don't think it! You can't afford to let negative, doubtful,
fearful, lustful, depressing thoughts run rampant in your mind.
Shut those thoughts down quickly before they take root in
your heart. I know it can be hard to do when your thoughts
are screaming at you, but the choice must be made not to
surrender to your old destructive way of thinking. Be selective
with your thoughts; your life depends on it!

*Now your attitudes and thoughts must all be constantly
changing for the better. Yes, you must be a new and
different person, holy and good. Clothe yourself with this
new nature.*
Ephesians 4:23-24 (TLB)

Let me be very clear by saying the devil is the one who puts
those negative thoughts in your mind, not God. However, you
are the one who has the choice in how you will handle those

bad thoughts, either receiving them or rejecting them. Second Corinthians 10:5 tells us "to take captive every thought to make it obedient to Christ." To take something captive is to capture and restrain it. When you decide to control your thoughts and not let them aimlessly wander in the wrong direction, then you will control the direction of your life. Have you ever had a thought or bad memory lead to another bad thought or memory, then another and another until you are drowning in sadness and regret? All of us have, but you can't allow yourself to go there. You must refuse to entertain adverse thoughts. You must immediately take that thought captive. Don't allow it to run freely through your mind. Seize it and capture it!

You actually have to discipline your mind to think good thoughts—God thoughts. It's easy to let your mind wander and focus on everything that is going wrong. You can't allow negative and self-defeating thoughts to influence your life anymore.

I have learned from Kenneth Copeland *you cannot change your thoughts with other thoughts, you must change your thoughts with words.* When those thoughts of shame or insecurity or worthlessness are trying to bring you down; speak against them. You might think it's crazy at first, but you must say out loud, "No, I do not accept that thought. I'm not going there!" That's why being in the Word of God is so important.

You can immediately start quoting what God says when those defeating thoughts try to come because it's already on the inside of you. If you start quoting what the Word says; it will immediately shut up the thoughts.

Verses like this become your weapons:

"I don't have a spirit of fear, but of power, love, and a sound mind"(2 Timothy 1:7).

"No weapon formed against me shall prosper" (Isaiah 54:17).

"I have been forgiven" (Ephesians 1:7).

"I am more than a conqueror" (Romans 8:37).

"I can do all things through Christ who strengthens me" (Philippians 4:13).

I'm not saying that if you quote a few scriptures all of the sudden life will become easy and you will never again feel unhappy or have a bad thought. No, but I am talking about a confident assurance that comes by faithfully spending time in His Word and being able to speak it out in times of need.

If you allow your bad thoughts to take over, not capturing them, they will try to tell you something better is "out there." We have all heard that saying, "The grass is always greener on the other side," but it's not. Believe me; I've been there, and it's not. When you start thinking about peaking over the envy "fence" for something better or different, it's usually a ploy to deceive and fool you into thinking, "over there" is better for you; when in truth, it usually harms you.

It all goes back to dying to self and taking "those thoughts" captive. Chasing after what looks good can become one of those choices that changes everything in your life for the worse. Be careful where you allow your thoughts to go; letting your wrong thoughts take over can be dangerous. Maybe your husband doesn't appreciate you the way you want him to, so you start talking to that old boyfriend online because you think he understands you better. Now you catch yourself laying in bed at night next to your husband, thinking of the other man.

It all began with a thought.

Your thoughts have misled you to think he will treat you the way you deserve to be treated. You have now become disillusioned and dissatisfied with what you have, fantasizing about what you don't have. In reality, there was a reason you and that guy broke up back then, but your thoughts and memories are enticing you along; causing you to forget. Your thoughts have now steered you into possibly making a terrible choice. Shut it down now before your thoughts take over and dictate your actions.

Your thought life is so important that the Bible warns us not to act thoughtlessly without regard. Whatever you think on the most determines the way your life will go. Decide right now to fix your thoughts on what God would want you to think on.

When worry tries to take over your thought life because it seems everything is falling apart around you and there is nothing else you can do: rest knowing that God is in control and will always take care of you. Stop trying to figure it all out by worrying.

Rest. Isn't that a wonderful word?

Oh, how I love the word *rest*. I think it's one of my favorite words. Being a mother of six, rest is a luxury that I rarely experience. But having peace of mind is the best rest of all. We read this verse in chapter one, but it's worth repeating here. Jesus said in Matthew 11:28, "Come to me, all of you who are weary and carry heavy burdens, and I will give you rest" (NLT). Learning how to let God be in control and live in that place of rest that Jesus offers, even when everything seems to be going wrong around you, is a must for true peace of mind. When you begin changing your thought life through the Word of God, great peace and joy comes in knowing that the Creator of the universe cares so very much for you!

> *Fix your thoughts on what is true, and honorable, and*
> *right, and pure, and lovely, and admirable. Think about*
> *things that are excellent and worthy of praise.*
> Philippians 4:8 (NLT)

You must be disciplined in your thought life. You can't let every thought that pops in your head be your first plan of action. Be selective. Be choosey.

Be picky about what you allow your mind to think on. Don't ever forget that your thoughts become your actions so chose your thoughts wisely!

Detours and Distractions

Have you ever been driving along and decided to take a road you thought would be a short cut, but instead, it made you late to your destination? Or, have you ever been curious about something you noticed on the side of the road and decided to pullover for a look? Be honest, have you ever followed a fire truck to see where the fire was? Those driving detours seem like harmless driving excursions, but like these detours of driving, the devil masterfully creates diversions in your personal journey, called life. He will show you a road that looks appealing and intriguing to your senses. Although you know your faith journey requires going the other way with your life, you just can't stop yourself and resist the enticing diversion. Beware! The signs along the way are colorful and alluring, which cause you to continue driving deeper and deeper down a winding and tangled path of sin. The farther you drive, the colors begin to fade to gray, the sun is now blotted out by the darkness and you are immersed in your terrible mistake. You were supposed to be on the "other" road, but somehow you became lost and can't get off this one. As the road becomes harder to see, you realize this isn't easy and fun anymore as when you first started out, and you have suddenly come to a complete stop. You discover you are stuck in mud and can't free yourself from the muck and mire of your self-created nightmare. It really doesn't matter anyway because you realize the road has come to a dead end. There is no where else to go because there is nothing there! You are suddenly faced with the fact that you were enticed down a wrong road that resulted only in a dead end for your life. You are all alone, stranded, and have wasted precious time and energy pursuing a road that fooled and lied to you. This is usually the time when you cry out for God to help, when He never wanted you to go down that road in the first place.

It seemed so innocent at first; your curiosity caused you to wander beyond this "boring" road you've been on. (The devil will try to convince you that walking the path God has for you is boring.)

You wanted excitement and you wanted a thrill, so you detoured off the steady path and went into what was only a set up—a detour and distraction for your life.

I watch my step, avoiding the ditches and ruts of evil so I can spend all my time keeping your Word. I never make detours from the route you laid out; you gave me such good directions.
Psalm 119 (MSG)

We have all been guilty of doing this at some time or another. We allow our flesh to decide our journey for life. Thankfully, because of God's great mercy and love for His children, He gets our lives turned around, and He leads us back to the peaceful road.

Never let your past failures and mistakes become your final destination.

We all have a course set by God. The worst place find yourself is going in the opposite direction of His set course. You are given opportunities throughout life, by the devil, to take those detours and diversions; to venture off another way. They mask themselves in many different forms. I know you can recall a time or two you've travelled the wrong way. The great deceiver comes in disguise to do anything to keep you distracted from the course that God has for you. Proverbs 4:25 says, "Keep your eyes straight ahead; ignore all sideshow distractions" (MSG).

Be aware and mindful of distractions; they are only meant to delay your destiny. Make a decision every morning to stay focused and on the right road for this day. There will always be crossroads in life, and you will have to decide to take the good and godly road or the road that calls to the flesh, leading to destruction of everything important in your life.

My child, listen to me and do as I say, and you will have a long, good life. I will teach you wisdom's ways and lead you in straight paths. When you walk, you won't be held back; when you run, you won't stumble. Take hold of my instructions; don't let them go. Guard them, for they are the key to life. Don't do as the wicked do, and don't follow the path of evildoers. Don't even think about it; don't go that way. Turn away and keep moving.
Proverbs 4:10-15 (NLT)

There might also be things (TV, social media, relationships, hobbies) not necessarily bad or sinful in your life, but they rob your time, energy, and focus and eventually become distractions. Be aware of those things too. They seem trivial, but don't allow them to sidetrack you from what you should be doing. Distractions will eventually turn into procrastination and delays that convince you, "You can do that tomorrow."

I'll admit to you that while writing this book, I let things get in the way and distract me from God's purpose. They weren't sinful things, but things I had allowed to become more important that robbed my time when I should have stayed focused on finishing this book. The Lord dealt with me one day while listening to a Beth Moore CD. She said, "The world needs what you have." I knew right then I was allowing other things to waste my time instead of doing what God had told me to do—to help others with His message of restoration through my life story. The fact that you are reading this right now shows I made the decision to no longer allow distractions to steal my time!

Is there something in your life taking your time and distracting you from what you should be doing? It may not be a bad thing, but you have given it more time than you should? Re-adjust your priorities; don't let them distract you any longer. Get back on track and finish what you started! The devil *never* wants you reaching your full destiny; he wants to keep you pursuing the desires of your flesh and relying on him for your pleasures.

He's been fighting you all your life to keep you off the right path. He constantly tries to trip you up and get you following a different path from the one God has planned. Don't fall for the distractions, and don't follow the detours!

God has rescued us from dead-end alleys
and dark dungeons.
Colossians 1:13 (MSG)

Every one of us has a predestined course designed by God, so faithfully stay on the road that He has laid out for you. Do not allow your emotions and feelings to cause you to veer off to the left or to the right, regardless of how appealing it looks at that moment. Satan will dedicate himself to making sure you will have every opportunity to do so, but stay on the right course. You know you are not supposed to be dating that guy. You know he's not the right one, but you're lonely. You're being distracted, stay on the course! When you stay on the course, you don't have to try and make up for lost time.

> 66 BARRICADES AND BARRIERS
> SHOULDN'T STOP YOUR JOURNEY. 99
> *JESSE DUPLANTIS*

Regardless of how many times you have gotten off the road, (you may be on the wrong road now), God can faithfully put you right back where you need to be. In fact, God already knew the detours you would take, but they don't change the destiny he has predestined for your life. You just have to choose to get back on His course.

How thankful I am for His grace when I've taken those wrong roads. I've been there and done that, one too many times!

If you will acknowledge your mistakes and allow Him to be your navigation system, He will graciously lead you to your final destination. He will never lead you astray.

You're blessed when you stay on course, walking steadily on the road revealed by God. You're blessed when you follow his directions, doing your best to find Him. That's right—you don't go off on your own; you walk straight along the road he set. You, God, prescribed the right way to live; now you expect us to live it. Oh, that my steps might be steady, keeping to the course you set; Then I'd never have any regrets in comparing my life with your counsel.
Psalm 119 (MSG)

Making right choices causes you to take the right paths. Staying on God's course for your life will never lead you down a wrong road!

CHAPTER 3

Marvelously Made

You made all the delicate, inner parts of my body and knit me together in my mother's womb. Thank you for making me so wonderfully complex! Your workmanship is marvelous—how well I know it. You watched me as I was being formed in utter seclusion, As I was woven together in the dark of the womb. You saw me before I was born.

Psalm 139:13-16 (NLT)

This passage of scripture is my all time favorite! It proves, without a doubt, we have been marvelously and uniquely made just the way God wanted us to be. When you begin to realize the depth of this scripture and the reality of your great worth, it will break any insecurity and inferiority with which you have struggled. There should no longer be any doubt of your worth when you realize you were magnificently made on purpose, for this set time! I looked up the word "marvelous" and it means "causing great wonder" and "extraordinary." God sees each and every one of us that way!

You are His . . .

amazing,

astounding,

awesome,

breathtaking,

sensational,

spectacular, and

marvelously made child!

The scripture says "knit me together in my mother's womb" and "woven together." When I think of the words *knit* and *woven*, I picture a beautiful embroidered quilt with all its amazingly intricate detail. The materials are joined, interlocked, and united to make a beautiful and lovely piece of art. God purposefully knit and wove you together with splendid detail. Psalm 139:15 in the Amplified Bible says, "I was being formed in secret and intricately *and* curiously wrought (shaped), as if embroidered with various colors." Does that make you feel special or what? You were intricately designed!

Isn't it amazing to think that there is only one version of you in the entire world! Even down to your fingerprints, no two people have the same! You may have traits and characteristics like your parents, but you are custom designed and one of a kind! Some people say I look just like my dad, others say my mom, but there is only one Jerriann, and there is only one you!

God designed you specifically when He put you together with your unique gifts, talents, strengths, abilities, personality, and traits. He didn't mess up, and He didn't make a mistake when He created you. God doesn't make rejects or defects.

You are an original.

You are exceptional.

You are rare.

You are His prized possession.

You are irreplaceable.

He is so very proud of His workmanship. God smiles when He thinks of the day you were born. He knew He had created an exclusive when it comes to you. God's stamp of approval shines on you!

You know exactly how I was made, bit by bit, how I was sculpted from nothing into something.
Psalm 139:14-15 (MSG)

Most of the insecurity I dealt with started with the fact that early on, I never liked my personality. I lived tormented for years, battling with this inside. In my eyes, my sister had the "perfect" personality; she was more likable, she was sweet and nice. Anytime I was described, the adjectives bossy, bold, stubborn, and strong-willed were used. I would be yelling inside, "But I'm sweet too!" I hated my personality. I wanted to be quiet and gentle, but for whatever reason, God decided to make me bold and strong. In my opinion, quiet and shy people seemed better, and no matter how many times I tried to be quiet, I just couldn't! LOL! (I'm laughing out loud at myself right now!)

I had a teacher tell me one time, I was a whale, and all my friends were fish, and I swallowed them all up by being bossy. I really didn't get the whale/fish analogy at the time, but I guess I fell short of using my leadership skills affectively that day. I needed some more refining.

God made me exactly the way He wanted me to be. Of course, I still have a lot of improving to do, even at my age, like knowing when to be quiet or having my own way! Regardless, despite all of my imperfections, He's proud of me and He's proud of you! Just like the psalmist says, I am so wonderfully complex, and so are you!

Be content with who you are.
1 Peter 5:7 (MSG)

HAPPY TO BE ME!

Not liking myself had been the root of all the insecurities in my life. It had also been the driving force in my search for approval. Combined with the insecurity was the condemnation I felt for all the poor choices I had made. It was like adding fuel to the fire of my already flaming feeling of worthlessness. I finally grew so weary of being bound by this harassing and relentless weakness in my life that I had to change the way I saw myself. I had to see myself through God's loving eyes. It has taken me a very long time of working through the junk and removing the garbage from my thinking. In doing so:

I can now say, I am comfortable being me, and I like me!

That confidence only comes from knowing who I am in Christ. No, I'm not perfect (my kids can tell you that), and I am continually working to fix my imperfections, but low self esteem no longer hovers over me like a dark cloud. Insecurity no longer causes me to look down and assume people won't like me. I can walk confidently into a room full of people with my head held high, not in arrogance, but because Jesus has lifted my head and given me a self-love that only comes from Him. He has healed me.

But you, Lord, are a shield around me, my glory, the One
who lifts my head high.
Psalm 3:3 (NIV)

You may have thought before, *No one gets me* or *No one understands me*, both are lies. God gets you and understands you perfectly, because He made you in His image and His likeness. When you finally realize you are made exactly the way your Heavenly Father created you to be, it opens the door wide to freedom from insecurity and acceptance of your true self. It also slams the door on the devil and his attempts to keep you feeling insecure. Insecure people can never truly be all that God wants them to be. Secure people thrive at just being themselves. Don't go another day intimidated by someone else because you have bought into the lie that they are better than you in some way.

My six children are all so different. They all have their strengths and weaknesses. I love them all the same and would never want to change one of their personalities for another. I will admit there are some who have easier going personalities than others, but I love them just the way they are. That is the way our Heavenly Father sees us. He knows our strengths and our weaknesses, and He still loves us! Some of us may have a more challenging way about us than others, but that doesn't surprise God. He made you, and He's so proud of you. If we give our weaknesses to Him, He will always turn them around and use them to His glory. He can always make something out of nothing!

I have created you and cared for you since you were born.
Isaiah 46:3 (TLB)

Those of you who are parents, I encourage you to let your children know you don't just love them, but you "like" them and their personalities. Parents play the most important role in building confidence in their children. Kids shine when they know they are supported and celebrated for just being themselves! If you have more than one child, appreciate their different personalities, and don't try to fit them into a mold not made for them. Let them be who they are, and never make them feel less for being anything other than their true selves. If you have more than one child then you know, they can be raised in the same house and be completely different in personality. They can see things differently and respond to things differently. That's what makes their perspective unique. Yes, you may have a child who has an easier going, laid-back personality, while another one is intense and on the dramatic side (I have a few of each). But that's okay because it takes all kinds! Give them permission to develop and become who God intends them to be. Encourage their strengths, and help with restructuring their weaknesses. My mother used to say to me often when I had lead another boycott, riot, or food fight at school, "Oh Jerri, if you would just use your leadership skills in a positive way." As frustrated as she felt with me all those times, she recognized early on, I was a leader. Each child has a God-given identity. Proverbs 22:6 (AMP), "Train up a child in the way he should go and in keeping with his individual gift . . ." Each one of us was given an individual gift. When a child feels loved just the way they are it builds a confidence in them that allows them to avoid certain insecurities and setbacks because of low self esteem. They already have enough pressures dealing with approval from their peers. Let home be their safe place of acceptance. Respect and admire their uniqueness. Be your children's biggest cheerleader; it will help them be more confident in their everyday lives.

This world needs a variety of personalities. It would be a boring place if we were all just alike. My house would be a boring house if all my kids acted alike. I like the diversity in my home. I have serious children, athletic children, artistic children, funny children, and I love all the differences. God likes diversity in His family too, and that's why He created you with your particular personality. There are no favorites with God. We are all His favorites. He likes you just the way you are, actually, He loves you just the way you are!

Simply become who you are.

If you struggle with knowing how very special you are, it's time now to let the inner conflict go and like yourself. You have been captive to this draining anguish too long! I meet women all the time who deal with this struggle of not being content and confident. Knowing who you are in Christ not only makes you self confident, but it brings out "God confidence" in you. With "God confidence" on the inside, you become "fearless, afraid of no one and nothing" (Psalm 27:1 MSG).

Be happy being you.

Be authentic.

Be real.

Be you.

God made you just the way He wanted you, and there is nothing you can do about it, so accept it! The quicker you begin to grasp and understand just how very special you are, just the way you are, the less struggle you will have in dealing with your life and your relationships. Confident and secure people possess a rare quality of peaceful contentment within themselves. They value themselves; therefore making them a breath of fresh air to be around. Let fear go! Love and embrace yourself—every part of you!

And ye are complete in him.

Colossians 2:10 (KJV)

It's your responsibility to take what He has given you and become the best you you can be! Are you getting it? Do you understand how very special you are? When God looks at you, He approves of His masterpiece—you! You are complete and perfect in Him.

Don't Listen to Them

When you accept the truth of how much God loves you and how thrilled He is with you, His handiwork, then you need to learn how to ignore the damaging and hateful words that others may have spoken over you at some point in your life.

Words are powerful. They can wound, sting, and crush your soul if you let them. I'm sure you've heard that old saying, "Sticks and stones may break my bones, but words will never hurt me." That's a lie. Words hurt badly, especially when spoken by someone you love. You may have had a parent that said to you, "Why can't you be more like your brother (or sister)?" You may have had a teacher that made you feel dumb in front of the class, or you may have a spouse that ridicules you and puts you down. All the destructive words that have ever been spoken over you are just more schemes of the devil to try and keep you down and defeated. If he can get you to believe those words and carry them around with you the rest of your life, he has accomplished what he set out to do—defeat you! Take off the negative labels others have put on you. Don't let him win by believing the lies.

> *Words kill, words give life; they're either poison or fruit—*
> *you choose.*
> Proverbs 18:21 (MSG)

I've had some hurtful and crushing words spoken over me before, and many times I've allowed them to affect me to the point of giving up and believing them as truth. To others, I appeared to have a tough exterior, but inside, I would immediately be affected and take in those hurtful words people would say as "the final word." The only way I've been able to recover from the sting of painful words is to get in God's Word and find out what He says about me. You must do the same. It's the only way you heal from the hurt. You need to become so convinced of your worth to God that regardless of the names you have been called in your past, they no longer affect you. When you get in His Word, you will become stronger and more confident. You will become like the Apostle Paul when he said, "None of these things move (affect) me." (Acts 20:24)

When thoughts have tried to enter my mind of what "they" said about me, many times I've had to speak out loud to quiet my mind and say, "That's not what God says about me." You are what God says, not what the hateful words say. See yourself the way God sees you, and "they" will have no power over how you feel about yourself. Your worth and value should never be determined from what others say, only from what God says about you. God sees the inside of you, even if nobody else does.

The fear of human opinion disables; trusting in God
protects you from that.
Proverbs 29:25 (MSG)

Often times, people who speak hateful words struggle in their own lives and often take their inner pain out on others. You've heard the phrase, "Hurting people, hurt people"; well, it's true, and it happens all the time.

My daughter, Madison, experienced this recently. She started a new school and sat in what she thought an available seat in one of her classes. A girl became angry because supposedly it was "her" chair. She began to call Madison names, talking about her to another girl. Yes, over a chair! My daughter and I just had a conversation on the way to school that morning about how deciding to have a good attitude at the beginning of the day sets the course for the rest of your day. She recalled our conversation from earlier, (Yay! They are listening) and chose not to let it effect her. When she got in the car and told me about it, I said, "Well, obviously this girl has issues that have nothing to do with you. Just go out of your way to be kind to her, and pray for her." The next day in class, Madison noticed this girl's arms and realized right away that she was a cutter. The girl's irrational behavior over a chair all made sense now; she's hurting inside. Madison immediately felt compassion for her and has gone out of her way to show kindness. She's praying for her too. This is a real example of how hurting people try to inflict their pain on innocent bystanders with their words and actions. It all goes back to choices.

Will you let others painful words and actions resonate and take root in your heart as truth? Or, will you decide to shake it off and believe the real truth, what God says about you? Did you forget? You are precious and priceless!

Don't dwell on the negative opinion of others.

I've been around people from my old days, and they start talking about what a trouble maker or brat I was and the time I did this or said that. I was just fine when I got there, but soon I would start getting that feeling (there's that word, "feeling"), that "I'm a bad person," and "no one likes me" trying to steal my peace and joy. I have to choose: do I accept it or reject it? Have you ever had that happen? They have no idea what you've battled in your life to conquer those kinds of feelings, so don't allow them to take you there with those thoughts from your past. Say to yourself, "Nope, I'm not gonna receive this feeling of worthlessness. That's not me. I'm a great person, and people like me!"

You might be saying, "Well, quite honestly, it is true what they have said about me. I have been a failure," or "I have made a lot of stupid mistakes."

Ok, that might be the case, but it doesn't matter how many times you have messed up because today is a new day, and you are not a failure anymore! God's mercy and grace is new every day. What you did yesterday does not define or determine today. Remember you are forgiven! Your mistakes were thrown "into the depths of the sea" (Micah 7:19). You might get around people who want to bring up your past, but that old you has been washed in the blood of Christ. Just ignore the negative remarks, and let it roll off of you. People and their opinions of you are unpredictable and may change often, but God's opinion of you remains unchangeable. Regardless of the mistakes you've made, His love is unconditional. Focus on what He says about you rather than the flawed opinions of others.

> " SOMEONE'S OPINION OF YOU DOES NOT HAVE TO
> BECOME YOUR REALITY. "
> *LES BROWN*

Stop Comparing Yourself

In my quest to be free of insecurity and become completely confident, I have realized that comparing myself to others was a major stumbling block. It was something from which I had to break free. Most of us have been guilty of doing this in one way or another, questioning how we measure up to others.

To see yourself wonderfully made in God's image, you are going to have to stop comparing yourself and accept God's beautiful workmanship. When you compare yourself to others, you are really saying, "What God made was not good enough," which is so far from the truth!

God does not create mistakes; He creates masterpieces.

Jeremiah 1:5 (NCV) says, "Before I made you in your mother's womb, I chose you. Before you were born, I set you apart for a special work." Why continue comparing yourself when this scripture makes it clear, that God knew exactly what He was doing when He created you. He chose you and set you apart. You didn't grow up and God say, "Oh, wow! I didn't realize she would be like that!" No, He knew exactly how you would be, and He wants you to use your personality for the "special work" He has set apart for you. It's going to take your specific temperament, introvert or extrovert, to do those things for God in a way that only you can do them! Be confident in knowing you are just right! I have a friend who is extremely quiet, barely saying a word when we are together. I always joke with her about making me nervous because she's so quiet, wondering what she's thinking about me, while the loudmouth is rambling on! I know at times she thinks of herself as weak, but I admire her for who she is, and I see her having strength and quiet resolve. She is made exactly the way God wanted her.

Have you ever seen someone attempting to be something other than themselves? It's awkward and uncomfortable, and doesn't look right. It's like trying to fit a size 9 foot in a size 6 shoe. It just doesn't fit.

True self confidence shines through when you are comfortable in your own skin. Sometimes I haven't really fit in with the PTA, soccer mom types. I see them all made up, scarves around their necks, sipping their lattes, while discussing their newest handbag. It's just not me and doesn't feel right.

I don't even like coffee, and I don't wear scarves. LOL!

So rather than pathetically trying to "fit in" by being something I'm not, I've sat alone many times at my kids' events, sipping on my Slurpee and realizing I forgot to put make up on! That's just me, and I like me.

Comparing yourself to others comes from feeling inadequate, and feeling inadequate comes from insecurity, and insecurity comes from fear, and fear comes from your enemy, the devil! We know he is a thief, and his number one goal is to kill, steal, and destroy (John 10:10). He wants to kill your dreams, by stealing your confidence and destroying your future. If he can keep you continually comparing yourself to others, he can rob you of the good life! The devil wants you to stay crippled by inferiority and insecurity, never realizing the true greatness of you! He knows when you find out the truth, (that you are already everything God wanted you to be) then nothing will be able to stop you from fulfilling all God has for your life!

I spent too many years believing the lie. Maybe you have too. We've wasted enough energy on lies and now it's time to believe the truth! God's truth.

Remember, you are complete in Him (Colossians 2:10), which means you lack nothing!

Through Jesus . . .

You are capable, qualified, and equipped!

Keep your eyes <u>fixed</u> on Him, not on what everybody else is doing.

Don't waste anymore time comparing yourself to others.

Never again allow yourself to *ever* feel less than someone else. You are good enough! Capitalize on your strengths.

Don't allow your imperfections to be magnified in your head.

Don't focus any more on what you can't do; focus instead on what you can!

Don't let your weaknesses rule over you any longer.

Stop being so hard on yourself; everyone has something to work on.

Stop letting your insecurities delay your destiny.

Stop procrastinating because you think you're not qualified.

Stop questioning yourself and diminishing the gifts you possess.

Stop second guessing yourself.

Do you know there are things you can do that no one else can do quite like you? You may not even see it, but you possess great things so just be good at being you!

We will not compare ourselves with each other as if one of us were better and another worse.

Galatians 5:26 (MSG)

Let me interject: social media can have a huge influence on how we compare ourselves with others. Many times we look at someone else's life (or "profile page") and think they have it made. They may look like they have it all together; making us think our lives pale in comparison. We all know that person who seems to travel all the time to exciting places, while you never get to go anywhere, or that couple who seem to have the "perfect" marriage, while yours is barely hanging on. What their profile page fails to mention is that their credit card is now maxed out because of that dream vacation, and the seemingly perfect couple has been talking divorce for months but posed for a quick picture together. Those images didn't show the huge fight before, the bad report, or the repossession notice. Yet, we compare and wish we could be like them, not knowing the truth.

We may actually have it better than what appears to be reality.

Most people tend to put out to the public what they want others to think about them. We rarely show our ugly sides. If you are not careful, you could start comparing yourselves to what others show. I'm not saying that everyone is fake; I'm just saying that we really don't know the truth about other peoples' lives. We don't know what goes on behind closed doors. You have to stop comparing your life to someone else's and just be happy living yours. To be honest with you, this type of comparing is really a form of jealousy, resenting someone's successes and advantages, or what they have that you don't have. Ouch! I know that hurts, but it's the truth. We must resist comparing ourselves.

Often times our negative thoughts can try to make us dwell on all the things we don't have, causing us to become ungrateful for what we do have. Someone may have a car that runs perfectly fine and is paid for, but they start comparing their "old junker" to their friend's new muscle car and decide they too need a new car. So, they go out and get the latest model and now have payments to make just because they started comparing themselves and became ungrateful in their thoughts.

You can't get caught up in what other's have or what others are doing. There will always be someone who has a nicer house, better behaved kids, a better body, or more money than you.

But you know what?

Someone may be looking at your life and wishing they had what you have.

Don't look at what you don't have. Instead, dwell on the

good things going on in your life.

Your house may be small, but it's nice, and you're never late on a payment. You may not get to go on fancy vacations, but that yearly trip to grandma's house with the kids is always a memorable time. You may not have the body you did when you were 20 years old, but you have your health.

There are so many things to be grateful for!

Gratitude is the best attitude.

There is a very old hymn that says, "Count your blessings, name them one by one, Count your blessings, see what God hath done!" This goes back to your thought life. The enemy wants you to forget all the wonderful things God has done in your life. Instead he wants to get you complaining about what's not going right and what you don't have. When you begin to focus on what others have that you don't, you open a door to an ungrateful heart. Look around; you have plenty of things for which to be thankful. Choose to view your world through a grateful lens. Find peace in the life you have right now, and live it to the fullest!

Body Image

We women are the worst at comparing ourselves to other women and their "perfect" bodies. The tall ones want to be shorter, and the short ones want to be taller. The skinny ones want to add a little more here and there, and the heavier girls want to be skinny! It's a never ending cycle of comparison. When I was a teenager, I wanted to be 5'7". To me, that was the "perfect" height because one of my best friends, Tina, is tall and I wanted to be tall like her. Well, I never grew over 5 foot! Wait, let me correct that; I am 5 foot and a half! That half is *very* important to me! It is what it is, and sadly I had to come to the realization that I'm never going to be 5'7". I had to learn to accept I was the little one that every one patted on top of the head when they walked by. I've had people say after meeting me for the first time, "I thought you would be taller in person." My height is just part of who I am, and it doesn't even bother me anymore. I'm just "Little Jerri." I wouldn't be me if I was tall. This is exactly how I was supposed to be.

Have you struggled with your body image? Of course you have, you're a woman (sorry guys if you're reading this). You may be heavy and may have battled your weight for a long time now. You already know what you need to do to get in better shape and eat right, but love yourself in the process. If you never get to your desired size, you still have to love yourself.

You shouldn't start loving yourself once you have arrived at the "perfect" weight. You should love yourself right now, exactly the way you are, regardless of your shape and size—big, little, short, tall, frizzy hair, and everything else in between!

Struggling with body image is another one of the many strategies of the devil to keep you feeling down about yourself. It will keep you feeling intimidated and inferior to others, never allowing you to flourish with your individuality. Listen very clearly to what I'm about to tell you: You are beautiful. Did you hear me? You are beautiful. Say to yourself right now, "I am beautiful." Now believe it.

If you are tall; stand proud, don't slump those shoulders, and if you have curves, work those curves!

Have you ever seen a woman walking through the mall with an outfit on a couple of sizes too small? She has stuff hanging out everywhere, yet she holds her head up and walks with all kinds of confidence. She is feeling good, real good about herself! I am always in awe of that kind of confidence, but actually, that's how we should be walking around all the time (with the right fitting clothes on, of course). You should hold your head high with a big confident smile on your face.

Confidence says, "This is me, and I like me."

Confident people are attractive. They don't have to be the

most beautiful person in the room, but if they carry themselves in a way that they like who they are, it makes you want to be around them.

Stop looking at that birthmark you hate or the acne scars you have. Forget about the stretch marks. Embrace and love you!

I remember sitting with a friend of mine at a pool one time. I felt really self-conscious in my swimsuit because I had just had my fourth child, and I still hadn't gotten rid of all the pregnancy weight. My friend, being on the heavier side, has struggled with her weight. She is beautiful, but what impressed me that day was she never cut herself down or said a negative remark about her body the entire day. She appeared confident; she laughed and enjoyed herself. Meanwhile, I sat there covered up most of the time, worrying about my extra pounds. She was living life and enjoying it, while I was miserable.

We need to move on from being so focused on what we don't like about our bodies. How many times have we not enjoyed ourselves on a night out because we were so upset that our favorite jeans were too tight to wear, or how many times have we not been able to relax on vacation, too concerned about what we looked like in our swimsuits? Being so focused on what we don't like about our bodies causes us to miss out on life! My mother told me a funny story the other day, relating to this very thing. She said she was in her early 30s and dieting, trying to lose weight for a special trip she and my dad were taking. She said she remembers crying to my dad on the plane that she didn't make her goal weight of 108; she was only 110! It sounds funny now because she was tiny and practically weighed nothing, and yet those 2 pounds affected her to the point of tears! Many of us are guilty of not enjoying the moment because of something we don't like about ourselves.

Hey, just so you know, I'm preaching to myself right now too; because most of the time when someone snaps a picture of me, I immediately look at my BIG thighs. Honestly, I don't like them and have cried many times about the "saddlebags" on my thighs, but I'm tired of stressing about them. Let's together, start focusing on the good things. There has to be something about your body you like. Even If it's just one thing, be proud of that one thing, and stop comparing your body to somebody else's. Work what ya got!

Don't fall for what the fashion magazines say is "What's In" (Size 0, flawless skin, long, slender legs). You being you is what's in!

Ok, get up right now and practice that confident walk I mentioned earlier! You know, that girl in the mall! Be that girl who walks with all kinds of confidence and wants the world to know it! When you were young, did you practice faces or modeling poses in the mirror? I wanted to be Miss America and would practice my runway walk. Well, do it now, practice that confident look. There you go; get those shoulders back; put your best smile on and shine! Walk with confidence regardless of your size or whatever else you've struggled with regarding your body image. You are beautifully and marvelously made. No more holding your head down; carry yourself like you're worth something!

Why? Because you are!

Seriously though, The Apostle Paul said we are Ambassadors for Christ (2 Corinthians 5:20). When I think of an Ambassador, I think of a diplomat sent to represent someone important. Do you think an Ambassador walks with his head down, insecure and lacking confidence? Absolutely not! They walk with a certainty, an authority, and knowing they are worthy of respect. If we are Christ's Ambassadors, we should be carrying our selves the same way, with confidence and dignity. "But you are a chosen people, a royal priesthood, a holy nation, God's special possession" (1 Peter 2:9 NIV).

You are not only an Ambassador, but you are a child of the King! Romans 8:17 says we are, "Heirs of God, and joint-heirs with Christ." That makes you highly favored because you are royalty!

Now practice that confident walk again!

Your Gifts and Talents

God gifts each one of us with talents and abilities, but most of time, we focus on what we don't have or what we can't do. That goes back to what we talked about earlier with comparing ourselves. Let's now focus on the gifts and skills you possess. What has God gifted you with—what are you good at? Those things that just come naturally to you. It may seem insignificant to you because it comes so effortlessly.

It's not just a coincidence that you are naturally good at something; God put those giftings on the inside of you. Second Timothy 1:6 says, "Make full use of the gift that God gave you" (CEV). It goes on to say, "God doesn't want us to be shy with his gifts (vs. 7 MSG).

Are you a good writer or have great organization skills?

Are you a good communicator or excellent at sales?

Do you enjoy cooking or working with the elderly?

Does the challenge of working with numbers and figures come naturally to you?

There is a man I know who works for my dad's ministry, named Scott. He oversees all the maintenance and the grounds (and whatever else comes up). You name it; he can do it or fix it. He's amazing at what he does. He has no desire to be famous with the spotlight on him; he just loves his job, and he's passionate about it. He has tapped into his gifts and talents, and he uses them for God. What a great joy it is to see someone using their God given abilities and actually loving the profession they have. That's Scott.

I have always been a person who likes getting people together. I enjoy hosting book clubs and Bible studies in my home. I'm always the one planning lunch dates with girlfriends and reunions with family or former classmates. At times, I have felt frustrated and hurt because I was always the one getting everyone together, and I felt like no one else put in the effort. I would think, *Why don't my friends ever plan things? Why is it always me?*

Then I realized other people are challenged with hosting parties and get-togethers, but it comes naturally to me. I love bringing people together. It's something I'm good at and enjoy. It could be overlooked as no big deal, but it is a gift. So, I use my gift often.

What gift(s) have you overlooked? I encourage you to make a list of things you are good at.

Are you: Detailed? Organized? Creative? Handy?

The attributes that you have go hand and hand with your gifts and talents, which all connect to your purpose.

Ask those closest to you. They can tell you your gifts. I did this recently and some of the words my friends used to describe me, were "warm hearted," "inviting," "multi-tasker," "encourager," and very resourceful.

Aware or not, you are using your gifts every day. Pay attention, they are part of your purpose.

I have a cousin who loves animals. She picks up strays all the time. In fact, she carries dog food and water in her car just in case she comes across a stranded animal. She works with animal shelters and always encourages others to adopt an animal. She is compassionate and caring. God put that love in her. It's one of her giftings. So, it's not surprising that her profession happens to be in health care, taking care of others.

God uses every bit of your personality: your likes, your dislikes, your interests, and your passions; while infusing them into your calling. He has a special role designed for you!

Are you a smiler? Have you been told you smile a lot? My sister is a smiler; she just can't help it. Her smile has always attracted people. She can be in a store shopping and just her smile brings a welcoming look to someone. I have seen people immediately open up to her and begin telling her something they are going through in their lives. She's been able to bring an encouraging word or pray with them right there in the store, all because of her smile. Just your smile can be one of the gifts God gave you, so use that gift! (And if you're not a smiler naturally, start working on it. The effect it can have on someone is amazing. You have no idea what your smile can do to someone in need of kindness.) Make smiling one of your talents!

You don't have to be on a stage preaching to thousands of people or serving as a missionary in Africa to be used by God. The things we are drawn to and enjoy are our giftings. Each one of us is different; we have our own distinctive talents and abilities. That's what makes us unique. Your gifts and talents are needed. There is someone out there who needs what you have. No one can do it like you can. You will thrive in life when you discover your gifts, big and small, and begin using them.

God has given each of you a gift from his great variety of spiritual gifts. Use them well to serve one another. Do you have the gift of speaking? Then speak as though God himself were speaking through you. Do you have the gift of helping others? Do it with all the strength and energy that God supplies. Then everything you do will bring glory to God through Jesus Christ.
1 Peter 4:10-11 (NLT)

I challenge you to develop in those areas in your life that just come easy to you. Don't make light of them, but really tap into them. Those are your gifts. God gave you those abilities to use for His good and His purpose.

Don't allow yours gifts to be wasted and unused because you're so focused on what you can't do or because you feel unqualified in some other area. I don't focus on singing, because I'm not good at singing. I focus on getting God's message of hope out, because I'm good at talking! God has need of you and your uniqueness!

Don't focus on what you aren't, but what you are!

We all have a part to play in the body of Christ. No one is more important or less significant than the other. Just like our body, each part contributes in making us work properly. First Corinthians chapter 12 explains this best:

> The body of Christ has many different parts, just as any other body does. Suppose a foot says, "I'm not a hand, and so I'm not part of the body." Wouldn't the foot still belong to the body? Or suppose an ear says, "I'm not an eye, and so I'm not part of the body." Wouldn't the ear still belong to the body? If our bodies were only

an eye, we couldn't hear a thing. And if they were only an ear, we couldn't smell a thing. But God has put all parts of our body together in the way that he decided is best. A body isn't really a body, unless there is more than one part. It takes many parts to make a single body. That's why the eyes cannot say they don't need the hands. That's also why the head cannot say it doesn't need the feet. In fact, we cannot get along without the parts of the body that seem to be the weakest. God put our bodies together in such a way that even the parts that seem the least important are valuable. He did this to make all parts of the body work together smoothly (CEV).

Never again allow yourself to think your gifts and talents are small in comparison to someone else's. God has given each of us a significant place. Strengthen and develop your own unique giftings. Watch how far you can go when you focus on the greatness already within. You can't help but give out to others when you work within your own uniqueness.

Remember, someone needs what you have. Give out from your gifts and talents, and you will always receive an amazing sense of fulfillment back.

> 66 SOMEONE, SOMEWHERE, NEEDS YOU—
> IN ALL OF YOUR UNIQUENESS—
> TO STEP UP TO THE PLATE OF YOUR CALLING. 99
> *PRISCILLA SHIRER*

Don't Say That!

Now that you know without a doubt how marvelously made you are in God's image and He loves you just the way you are, it's now time to stop talking down to yourself. No more cutting yourself down with negative talk. Enough already! From here on out, you *only* speak good things about yourself. If a negative remark slips out, immediately replace it with a positive word! Here are just a few words to remind you of your greatness:

smart	unique
capable	special
incredible	brave
amazing	loved
terrific	wonderful
exceptional	cheerful
talented	strong
beautiful	faithful

You get the idea now? No more "ouch" words. You would never tolerate someone talking down with cutting words to your child. So, why do it to your Heavenly Father's child? He doesn't like it when you speak down about yourself. Speak words of love and approval over yourself. The Bible says, "You have what you say" (Mark 11:23 NCV). You believe yourself more than any other person. Look in the mirror when you get ready to start your day, and say to yourself, "Wow! You're beautiful! You're going to do amazing things today!"

Your thoughts are powerful! Your words are powerful!

66 NEVER AGAIN SAY AN UNKIND WORD ABOUT YOURSELF. 99
JOYCE MEYER

The more you say kind and encouraging words about yourself, the more convinced you will be. Eventually you will become what you say—everything listed above and then some!

CHAPTER 4

I Forgive Me

He saved us because of his mercy, and not because of any
good things that we have done. God washed us by the
power of the Holy Spirit. He gave us new birth and
a fresh beginning.
Titus 3:5 (CEV)

All of my life I have known that when I confessed my sins to
Jesus, He forgave me immediately and washed them away.
Despite having that knowledge, I still carried with me shame
and sorrow for all the bad decisions and poor choices I had
made in my life (just another side effect of having low self
esteem). If a bad memory of a sin I had committed would
come back to my mind, I would go back to God and ask Him
to forgive me *again*. Yet, the Bible clearly explains that once
you have asked God to forgive you, He forgives right then.
Obviously, God didn't need to forgive me; I needed to forgive
myself. Have you been guilty of doing this? If so, than it's
an indication that you have not forgiven yourself for your
mistakes. That's what condemnation is; it judges and makes you
feel guilty when God has already forgiven you.

He has removed our sins as far from us as the east
is from the west.
Psalm 103:12 (NLT)

Often times, we become our greatest enemy because we cannot forgive ourselves and continue to hold on to our past sins still lurking deep within. We battle inwardly with issues and events from our past that have already been forgiven by God the instant we asked Him.

When you continue to hold onto your past,
you allow your past to control you . . .
having a say-so in your life.

When you don't forgive yourself, it cripples you and never allows you to move forward toward the future. Remembering your past keeps you forever bound to your yesterdays by keeping your mistakes in the forefront of your heart and mind. You can only move forward when you stop looking back. You can't take your past into the future and expect to fulfill God's purpose for your life. For true healing and restoration to occur in your life, you must forgive yourself and move beyond the past memories and the past shame.

All the earlier troubles, chaos, and pain are things of the
past, to be forgotten. Look ahead with joy. Anticipate
what I'm creating.
Isaiah 65:17-18 (MSG)

The Sacred Shoebox

I had this old shoebox full of mementos from my past, and every time I moved, I carried it with me. From Texas to California, on to Colorado, and then back to Texas—it always went with me. It stayed safely tucked away with my photo albums and childhood memorabilia. I didn't dare open the shoebox because it represented places I didn't want to go back to in my mind. It was too painful. Yet, it continued to stay with me, year after year. For some reason, I didn't want to let go of it. The shoebox was not only a part of my belongings, but had become a part of me.

Recently I began purging in preparation to sell our home, and I found the shoebox. I don't think it had been opened in ten years or more. I was finally brave enough to open it and see what was in store for me from my painful past. I waited until I was alone and carefully opened the lid in apprehension that all the memories and hurt would come pouring out on me. Piece by piece, I went through every item in awe that this sacred box of nothingness had followed me everywhere.

There was nothing in it that meant anything to me anymore. The mementos, ties and connections to my past, were no longer there. I ripped and tore everything into tiny pieces and threw the entire box in the garbage where it belonged. It was something that I should have been done many years ago. It was a wonderful feeling. I couldn't believe I had carried this box of the past around with me for so long, and yet it meant so little to me. I was free! The memories and the shoebox had no hold on me any longer! God had forgiven me of my past, and so had I. What freedom that is!

> 66 LET GO OF WHAT DOESN'T MATTER. 99
> *CHRISTINE CAINE*

The shoebox represented so much to me that day I threw it away. I started thinking about how often we carry our mental shoeboxes around with us. Perhaps there are things we've done that we have never forgiven ourselves for and yet we keep them tucked away in our minds. Or maybe there are things that should have been dealt with and thrown away long ago that we continue to hold on to. It's time to get rid of the residue from your past.

If God can forgive us of the many wrong things we have done, then we must forgive ourselves. The Apostle Paul says,

I focus on this one thing: "Forgetting the past and looking forward to what lies ahead" (Philippians 3:13-14 NLT). If Paul could forget his past, a man who called himself the worst sinner of all (1 Timothy 1:15 CEV), then don't you think you can forgive yourself of your past? Imagine . . . if after Paul's miraculous experience on the road to Damascus (see Acts 9), he had continued to replay in his mind all the bad things he had done by persecuting Christians and had been unable to forgive himself? What if he had said, "I just can't get over all the horrible things I've done."

The majority of the New Testament would have never been written if Paul had chosen to hang onto his past, never forgiving himself. For centuries, his writings have had an impact on millions and millions of people. It came down to a choice he made, "Forgetting the past and looking forward to what lies ahead." He redirected his focus and passionately went about doing what God had preplanned for his life, regardless of his horrible past.

Get rid of your old shoebox—those shoes don't fit anymore!

Forgiveness is a letting go. Imagine walking around with heavy books in your hands. Every where you went, you carried this very high stack of books with you, but one day someone told you, "You don't have to carry those around; just drop them." That's how you should see your sins. The things from your past you've done that you're not proud of, and those horrible things that have been done to you are old baggage, dead weight that can easily be dropped. Now feel how light and easy your load has become. It's just that simple. You no longer have to carry around that heavy load of shame and guilt. You are free to be yourself without condemnation and guilt. Hebrews 12:1 (KJV) says, "Let us lay aside every weight, and the sin which doth so easily beset us . . . " Put aside everything you have ever done wrong and see yourself as clean, free, and forgiven having a fresh beginning.

Take your promiscuity,

your abortion,

your cutting,

your self-hatred,

your anger,

your divorce,

your addictions,

your bad choices, or

whatever else you've been carrying around . . .

and lay them at the feet of Jesus.

See Him hanging on the cross for *your* sins. He died for you! See His blood pouring over your sins and washing them clean from your life. Let Him not only take the sin, but the pain, the guilt, the shame that came with it. Give Him anything and everything associated with your past life. Galatians 3:13 (MSG) is so powerful. It says, "Christ redeemed us from that self-defeating, cursed life." Maybe you've made a complete mess of things, and you're tired. Why don't you lay it all down now and get free from a self-defeating, cursed life?

Our old way of life was nailed to the cross with Christ, a decisive end to that sin-miserable life—no longer at sin's every beck and call!
Romans 6:6 (MSG)

I think now is a good time to ask you: have you made Jesus the Lord of your life yet? If not, what are you waiting for? No more carrying around the past with you. Today is the day to release it once and for all and know you are forgiven. When Jesus died on the cross for you, He took every pain, every weakness, every sin you ever committed! Through the death of Jesus, God's Son, you were bought with a great price, and your debt has been paid. God loves you just how you are right this very moment. He's not waiting for you to be perfect. He wants you to come to Him just as you are. He doesn't see you as trash or worthless. He doesn't look at the mistakes; He sees the potential. He sees greatness. You are very valuable in His eyes! He sees every tear you've ever cried. Let Him wipe them away for good. He can bring light to your darkness, strength to your weakness, and hope to your discouragement.

Say this prayer with me:

"Heavenly Father, I ask you now to cleanse me and forgive me of the mistakes I have made and all the sin I have committed. Jesus, come into my heart and be my Lord and Savior now. Take the hurt and pain from my past. Create in me a clean heart. Thank you for dying on the cross for me and giving me a new life. From this day forward, I will follow after Your will and Your ways for my life, in Jesus' name, Amen."

Aah, doesn't that feel good?! It's that simple. You are forgiven! Now you have to see yourself as someone who has never done anything wrong! You are like a new born baby, innocent of sin. Shame is no longer a part of you. You are no longer the "old" you anymore. You are a brand new person because of Jesus! When your mind wants to replay the horrible things you've done or the stupid decisions you've made, you just say, "I don't know who you are talking about. That's not me anymore!"

You are free, and you are forgiven in Jesus!

Forgiveness brings a whole new confidence. Walk away from your sins and your past, never pick it up again, and never look back.

> *The person who knows the meaning of forgiveness, who is*
> *no longer plagued by past failures, who stands blameless*
> *and guilt-free before God, that person is rich indeed.*
> Psalm 32:1-2 (Psalms Now)

One of my favorite Bible illustrations of this amazing forgiveness we've been offered is found in the eighth chapter of John. The religious scholars of the day brought a woman before Jesus, caught in the act of adultery. They tried to embarrass and humiliate her in front of everyone. The law said she was to be stoned for such an act. Notice it was the religious scholars, "The know it alls" that felt it was their duty to inform Jesus of her sins. (I've met some Christians like that too. Ones that feel it's their duty to judge, condemn, and inform others.) They kept waiting for Jesus to respond to this horrible sin, yet he just knelt down, writing in the dirt. Jesus stayed cool and calm, while they tried to trap Him and ridicule her in the process. Finally, He responds to them and says,

"All right, but let the one who has never sinned throw the first stone!"

One by one, they all began to walk away. The part I love the most is when Jesus stands up and faces the woman eye to eye and says to her, "Where are your accusers? Didn't even one of them condemn you?"

She replies,

"No, Lord."

Then Jesus says to her,

"Neither do I. Go and sin no more."

It's as simple as that.

He didn't say to her, "Oh, that sin is just too big for me to forgive. You have made so many mistakes; I can't forgive you." He wasn't shocked or disturbed in the least, yet He moved with love and compassion. He looked beyond the sin and simply forgave. He basically said, "I forgive you for what you've done. Now, get on with your life, and don't do it anymore." There was no condemning, no going over all the details of her sin, just love in its purest form. Jesus treated her like a person of significance. He saw her worth, not her sin. That's what He is saying to you today, "I forgive you, now forgive yourself; don't do it anymore, and let's get on with life!" He sees your worth too.

Anyone who belongs to Christ has become a new person.
The old life is gone; a new life has begun!
2 Corinthians 5:17 (NLT)

No Regrets

There are so many crossroads I've taken in life and later wished I had gone another way instead of the path I chose. If you are like me, you may have allowed regret to creep in when you look back at your life and see all the years and opportunities wasted. How many times have we said, "If I had only known then, what I know now." Regret robs you of living in the now and enjoying life to the fullest. There is nothing we can change about our past, it's already been done, so let it go. We can't live in the should've, could've, would'ves of life. They are all "time robbers" and "dream wasters."

Don't stumble over something behind you.

There is no point in replaying what could have been. Just the other day going through old photos, I started to feel that icky feeling of regret trying to creep over me, while looking through my life in pictures. Regret of failed marriages, regret of dumb decisions, regret of lost and wasted years. I had to make myself snap out of that miry fog and feel thankful for my life *now*. That's the old me, it's not who I am today.

When your mind wants to bring up the past and replay old sins, remember it's forgotten. That's the old you! You no longer think, speak, or act like your past. This is the new you! Forgiving yourself gives you the capability of having the relationship your Heavenly Father has desired to have with you. Others may remind you of your past mistakes, but Jesus *never* will!

Your past does not have to determine, define, or dictate your future!

Don't replay the past mistakes and lose precious time dwelling on what a horrible person you were and what horrible things you've done . . . get over it! Please know, I say that completely in love. I know first hand how the devil wants you to continually replay the scenes from your past. In Revelation he is called "the accuser of the bretheren." That's what he attempts to do, condemn you with fault finding accusations, beating you down with thoughts of past failures, failures that have long been washed away. Don't fall into the trap. You can never get anywhere always looking back. Don't let the images of your past continue to invade your thought life. It only delays you moving forward to God's bright future for you! Every day is a new day and a fresh start!

The faithful love of the Lord never ends!
His mercies never cease. Great is his faithfulness;
his mercies begin afresh each morning.
Lamentations 3:22-23 (NLT)

I read this quote the other day that said, "It's not what I have been through in my life that defines who I am. It's how I got through it that has made me the person I am today." That is so good! No matter what you've been through and what bad mistakes you've made in your past, they do not define you. It's what you do with life's experiences and how you grow and learn from them. It's not over just because you messed up!

> 66 IT IS NEVER TOO LATE TO BE
> WHAT YOU MIGHT HAVE BEEN. 99
> *GEORGE ELIOT*

Often times, we just settle for less in life. We think, "Well, I've messed up so many times. God would never use me." Pick yourself up, wipe yourself off, and get on with life. If you tripped and fell over something, would you lay there for days, months, or even years before you decided to get up? Of course not. But often times, we do it with our lives. We wallow around in the mud of life (our past) for years, wondering why we can't get ahead in life. It's time to get up, wash the past off, and get going again! God is able to get you right back on track from where you once left off. Joel Osteen says, "God can take you from pitiful to powerful."

You might say, "I'm just too old now." That is regret talking! You are never too old to start fresh. God still has plans for your life, regardless of your age. I've struggled with the age thing at times too, thinking I'm not getting any younger and yet knowing I'm called to be in full time ministry. The thoughts have come that I've wasted so much time on those detours set by the enemy. I know those thoughts are just lies from the devil, trying to bring regret and sorrow.

> 66 YOU ARE NEVER TOO OLD TO SET ANOTHER
> GOAL OR TO DREAM A NEW DREAM. 99
> *C.S. LEWIS*

My grandmother, 84 at the time of me writing this, is such a huge inspiration to me. Her age means nothing to her; it's just a number. Nothing stops her; she lives in the now. My last time with her, she talked about adding on to her home, and when I talk about adding on to her home, I'm talking about her and her family actually out there doing the labor themselves. (She's a country girl and knows how to work!) Her age doesn't stop her, and it shouldn't stop you! Don't let that be a regret any longer in your life. My grandmother quotes this scripture every time I see her, "My youth is renewed like the eagle's" (Psalm 103:5).

Do you think God looks at you and is thinking, "Oh, she is just too old now. I could never use her!" No, He sees your purpose! Let me remind you that Sarah gave Abraham a son at 90, and he was 100 years old. Noah built the ark at 600 years old when the flood came, and you are regretting turning 50 this year! Please! You are never too old to thrive!

God doesn't see your age. He sees your purpose.

It's time to live in the now. Every moment is a moment you will never get back, so do something now with your life. Close the chapter on the old life, and begin a new one. You are the author of your story. You cannot live your life looking back and wondering. There is no fruit in the "wondering," only in the living and doing! You have lots of life still in you! No more excuses.

Forget about what's happened;
don't keep going over old history. Be alert, be present.
I'm about to do something brand-new.
Isaiah 43 (MSG)

I Forgive Them

You may have grabbed hold of the fact that God has forgiven you now, you might have also released the past to forgive yourself, but you may still be struggling with all the pain inside because of what others have done to you. You are still hurting because your heart has been broken. The pain is so deep. It has crushed you and wounded you immensely as if you've been punched in the gut. Oh, I know that kind of pain. They hurt you so badly; you wonder if you'll ever get through it and get over it. There is a hole in your heart that never seems to close. Do you relive the betrayal, the abuse, or that horrible scene that is deeply embedded in your soul? Some pain has been down on the inside of you for so very long that it's roots have grown so thick around your heart; now anger has replaced the hurt. You know exactly what I'm talking about because you thought of it immediately. It goes everywhere with you and lingers often in your thoughts. This pain eagerly awaits an opportunity to be brought up. It relishes in being replayed over and over again in your mind or with others who will let you tell it again. It wakes up with you and goes to bed with you.

Aren't you tired of being angry?

Isn't it time to forgive?

Jesus can heal your broken heart and take away the anger that came with it. You think the walls you've built around your heart are protecting you, but they are only hurting you by keeping you bound inside them, with the tormenting thoughts beating you down of what was done to you. Tear those debilitating walls down! You are not going to like to hear this, but you are going to have to forgive the person/people who have hurt you. You will never truly be free until you do. You can't keep holding on to it and carrying it with you. Unforgiveness turns into bitterness when not dealt with, and it's costly. It binds and restricts, not the person who caused the pain, but you! It robs you of the life you should be living, and it can also cost you your health. I know it's hard, and you are probably thinking, *You have no idea what they did to me. It was bad. It was wrong. It was not my fault.*

I know your pain is very real, but to move forward; you **must** forgive that person who hurt you. Forgiveness is not accepting or condoning someone else's bad behavior; it's a freeing and letting go on your end, refusing to allow that person and their wrong actions to no longer have control over you.

Don't ruin a good today by thinking about a bad yesterday. Let it go.

Only through God's help can we forgive those who have wounded us greatly. You can no longer see yourself as the victim. Don't give them that power in your life anymore.

Let the hateful words go.

Let the neglect go.

Let the abuse go.

You can't do it on your own. No amount of positive thoughts or will power has been able to relinquish this pain. No amount of drinking it away or shopping 'til you drop" has been able to medicate it. You may have tried other things to take the pain away—alcohol, drugs, relationships, or any other addiction—but those are just temporary pain relievers. Take back your life now, and receive your freedom through Jesus. He can give you permanent healing of your broken heart, but you have to give Him all the pieces first.

Luke 4:18 tells us, He was sent "to heal the brokenhearted, to preach deliverance to the captives, and recovering of sight to the blind, to set at liberty them that are bruised."

Is that you: Broken? Captive? Blind? Bruised?

He can restore (make new) your soul. "Your great power is sufficient to set me free from these things that hurt my soul" (Psalm 21, Psalms Now). Your soul is your mind, your will, and your emotions. Jesus can take the memories of what "they" did and heal your mind. He can give your mind peace that washes away all the hurt of the past. Only Jesus can do this.

When I was a little girl going through something hard for me at the time, I would go and sit on my daddy's lap. He would hug me and say,

"Everything will be okay; Daddy will take care of it."

I remember the comfort it would bring when he spoke those words. It would make everything better. I would take a deep breath because I just knew, somehow, some way, my daddy would do everything in his power to make it all better for me. I knew with my dad on my side, I could get through anything. It's the same way with your Heavenly Father. You need to see Him as a loving Father who adores you and only wants the best for you. Picture yourself crawling up in His lap right now and hear Him say,

"Everything is going to be okay. Daddy will take care of it."

Let His love heal your heart and pick up the broken pieces of what has been done to you in the past.

He heals the brokenhearted and bandages their wounds.
Psalm 147:3 (NLT)

I know from my own experience, this one person hurt me repeatedly. I had gone to God in prayer and made a choice to forgive them, but the memory of the offense would resurface over and over again in my mind. If I played into what the devil was scheming by bringing the memories back, then I would begin to dwell on what they did again. I would become angry all over again, and the horrible cycle would begin. I finally realized through the process of forgiving others that it doesn't bother God how many times you may need to go to Him when the memory of the pain tries to return. God knows your heart, and He knows you want to be free of this unforgiveness.

If what they did tries to come back in your mind fifty times a day, then you will have to say fifty times a day, "I have already forgiven them. I will not think on bad things. I choose to think on good things." You take it to Him as many times as you need to until you are free. Refuse to dwell on the past; instead, dwell on the forgiveness.

Give all your worries and cares to God, for he cares
about you.
1 Peter 5:7 (NLT)

Jesus gave us a powerful gift that can help in any time of need. This gift helps us when we cannot help ourselves. When the burden is too heavy and the load is too much, this gift is here for us anyway we need Him to be. This amazing gift is the indwelling power of the Holy Spirit.

You might be saying, "What in the world are you talking about? Let me explain.

In John chapter 14, Jesus speaks to His disciples before He is betrayed by Judas and arrested. He tells them of the Holy Spirit whom He will leave with them after He is gone. The Greek word for the Holy Spirit is *Paraclete*, which means advocate or support. Once received, the Holy Spirit comes in and dwells in us, becoming our Comforter, Counselor, Helper, Intercessor, Strengthener, and Standby. When I have not been able to cry another tear and have felt like no one cares, I know the Holy Spirit is there for me. When I have not been able to let what "they" did go, the Holy Spirit has been there to help me. The Holy Spirit can help you release all the anger and all the unforgiveness you've been carrying around.

He comforts you.

He helps you.

He strengthens you.

He empowers you.

The Holy Spirit is available to those who believe Jesus is Lord. Ask Jesus now to fill you with His Holy Spirit, and let Him be everything you need Him to be in your life.

When you are feeling confused, let Him be your *Counselor*.

When you are feeling weak, let Him be your *Strengthener*.

When you need a defender, let Him be your *Advocate*.

When you need consoling, let Him be your *Comforter*.

But the Holy Spirit produces this kind of fruit in our lives: love, joy, peace, patience, kindness, goodness, faithfulness, gentleness, and self-control.
Galatians 5:22-23 (NLT)

The Holy Spirit gives us *everything* we need to live a content and satisfied life:

Love that is secure and unconditional.

Joy that is full.

Peace even in the storms of life.

Patience when every one else is not.

Kindness when you don't feel like being nice.

Goodness in a bad world.

Faithfulness when you've never been faithful.

Gentleness when you need to be gentle.

Self-control when everything else is out of control.

He is everything you need. You can't stay angry anymore when you let the Holy Spirit in your life. You can't keep hanging on to the pain when the Holy Spirit becomes your helper.

I honestly cannot imagine my life without the Holy Spirit. When I have been completely helpless with no idea what to do or how to pray, I go to the Holy Spirit and ask Him to help me. He shows me how to be a godly woman, a good mother, a wise money manager and provides any help I might need. Don't go another day trying to do it all on your own. Haven't you already proven you stink at trying to figure it out on your own? I know I have! Let the Holy Spirit fill you with love, joy, peace, patience, kindness, goodness, faithfulness, gentleness, and self-control to live a victorious life.

CHAPTER 5
Finding True Love

Many of us grew up singing "Jesus loves me, this I know, for the Bible tells me so." but do you really, really, really know just how much He loves you? It's a love that no human being is capable of giving. It goes beyond anything we have ever experienced from another person. No matter what you've done or how bad you've acted or will act, this love cannot be taken away from you. Unlike most people's love, God's love is not based on conditions; it's unconditional and never ending! People can change and their love can wane, but God remains changeless in His love for you.

And I am convinced that nothing can ever separate us from God's love. Neither death nor life, neither angels nor demons, neither our fears for today nor our worries about tomorrow— not even the powers of hell can separate us from God's love.
Romans 8:38 (NLT)

When the scripture says "Nothing can separate us from God's love," it really means what it says . . . nothing! His love for you is not based on your perfection or performance. His love is not based on what you did or how you acted. He just loves you. He is love.

Period. That kind of love brings a security and confidence that no one else can ever give you.

Doesn't it bring peace to your heart and mind, knowing that God loves you that way? It does mine! There was a period in my life when I had messed up so badly, letting so many people down. In fact, some people turned the other way when they saw me. The only thing that got me through that dark time was the truth I held on to in knowing, "Nothing can ever separate me from God's love." Those words sustained me and kept me going while my soul was being restored. Despite my shortcomings, my weaknesses, my stupid decisions, He still loves me.

When you truly fall in love with Jesus and no longer allow the "joy of your salvation," or the joy of knowing Him to be lost, you will find "The Greatest Love of All" (but even better than a Whitney Houston song)! When you fall in love with Jesus, you can't help but love yourself too!

> *Restore to me the joy of your salvation, and make me*
> *willing to obey you.*
> Psalm 51:12 (NLT)

No one had the ability to make me feel better about myself until I made a complete surrender to Jesus. I found joy in my relationship with Him again, something I had taken for granted for too long . . . until I needed it so desperately.

Jesus is quite capable of giving you all the love you need. There is no greater relationship than the one you have with Jesus. He gives all the peace, all the comfort, all the security, all the joy—everything you need! When you finally get fed up with failing at love, then and only then will you find your true love in Him. Let Him become your safe place, your refuge from the storms of life.

The love of God is complete, which means it's whole, it's absolute, and it's perfect. The more you seek after Him, the more He fills you. He becomes your life source. The approval from others begins to dim in comparison to His great love for you.

You may be single right now after several failed relationships, wanting to finally settle down with the right one. I encourage you to focus on putting Jesus first before anything else in your life; pursue seeking Him; let Him bring the right person to you. Don't get caught up in the rat race of trying to find the "perfect" one. That kind of life leads to too many unnecessary detours and distractions. Just give it to God, and let Him take care of all that. He knows and cares about your heart's desire. If you are traveling His path for your life, He will bring that right person across your path. Focus on God's love for you, and trust His plan . . . instead of your own.

As the deer longs for streams of water, so I long for you, O
God. I thirst for God, the living God.
Psalm 42:1-2 (NLT)

Falling in love with Jesus has not only allowed me to love myself, but it has made me a better woman, a better mother, and a better friend. It has taught me how to love the way Jesus loves. I'm definitely still a work in progress, but with God's help, I am now capable of being in a relationship without being so needy and selfish. I am able to give back and not expect so much in return. No more self-hatred, no more comparing myself, no more insecurity; just complete acceptance of His great love for me.

There is a song by Jesus Culture that says, "Your love never fails, never gives up, never runs out on me." I can't tell you how many times I've played that song, reminding me of just how loved I am by God.

Immerse yourself in His love for you. Find out how great and how wonderful it is.

I finally found my acceptance and my affirmation in His love. That's the answer. He has been there all along, waiting to be my partner for life.

All those tears I cried, He was there holding me.

All the brokenness I felt, He was there to restore me.

All the pain I felt, He was there to heal me.

All the sleepless nights, He was there to comfort me.

He was always there.

My self-worth does not come from a man anymore; it comes

from Jesus. My stability does not come from being in a relationship anymore; it comes from Jesus. My approval does not come from others; it comes from Jesus.

It took me long enough to realize, that in my relationship with Him - Jesus has become my everything! I have found true love in my Savior. He has turned my life around and is using it to exemplify His amazing love, mercy, and restoration for His child.

No more searching . . .

searching for love

searching for acceptance

searching for security

searching for identity

I am finally settled in my heart.

The time has come to start looking to Jesus to be your everything.

My sweet friend, I can't tell you enough how much He loves you.

He waits to be your true love.

He will never abandon you.

He will never turn His back on you.

He will never break His promises.

He will never love you with conditions.

He will always love you no matter what.

He is there right now, waiting for you.

Fall into His arms and allow Him to be the lover of your soul.

Jesus, Lover of my soul,

Jesus, I will never let you go

You've taken me from the miry clay

You've set my feet upon the Rock, and now I know

I love you, I need you,

Though my world may fall, I'll never let you go

My Saviour, my closest friend,

I will worship you until the very end

(Hillsong Music)

Falling in love with Jesus brings a wholeness to your life that no other relationship can bring. Falling in love with Jesus brings a validation and acceptance you may have been looking for your whole life. He sees you. He hears you. He accepts you. You don't have to pretend to be anything other than your authentic self. He loves you dearly.

I Love You Too

When you begin to allow the love of God to envelop your whole self, then you become capable of loving others in a healthy way. You are no longer half of a person looking to be loved, but a whole person capable of giving love.

When you make God's love your aim, then the law of sowing and reaping comes into play—you give love; you receive love. The hardness of your heart crumbles and allows you to freely express love, because God's way of loving (the purest form of love) has taken over. There is no motive involved when you love God's way. It is not selfish. Loving others is no longer out of a need to get love back, but an overflow from God's love in you. It becomes easier to understand the true meaning of giving love.

"Love is patient, love is kind, it isn't jealous, it doesn't brag, it isn't arrogant, it isn't rude, it doesn't seek its own advantage, it isn't irritable, it doesn't keep a record of complaints, it isn't happy with injustice, but it is happy with the truth. Love puts up with all things, trusts in all things, hopes for all things, endures all things. Love never fails."
I Corinthians 13:4-8 (CEB)

CHAPTER 6

It's Not Over Yet!

All my life, my dad has repeatedly said to our family, "Savelles aren't quitters!" I just knew I must have been accidentally placed in the wrong family because it was hard for me to live by those words. (I knew I was in the right family, because I look just like my mom.) But quitting is what I did all the time when things got hard. You know those really optimistic people who just love challenges and feel inspired by conquering obstacles when they arise? Well, I wasn't one of them. I wanted to quit at the smallest amount of pressure. Often times I did with relationships and commitments I had made in my life. I let people down, I let myself down, and I let God down every time I decided to throw in the towel. In 2007, I hit rock bottom. I quit *big time* and failed miserably. I had let the devil deceive me, and I fell hard . . . hook, line, and sinker for his lies and deceptions. I committed adultery and left my husband. I turned my back on everyone and everything I had worked passionately for. The devil had me just where he wanted me. *Once again*, I lived up to the labels of "Jerri the failure," "Jerri the loser," "Jerri the quitter." My world had completely fallen apart. The phone was silent because most of my friends had no idea what to say, so I was all alone in the reality of what I had done. Night after night, I laid in the darkness of my tiny new apartment in the aftershock of my new life. Stunned and dazed, I asked myself repeatedly:

Why did I do this?

How could I have let this happen?

The truth and reality was, I knew it had all come down to my thought life, which led to *my* choices. I had let it happen. I had not shut the door on temptation. I had let bitterness and resentment towards another person (who wasn't even my husband) take root in my heart. The devil knew where to hit me the hardest—another broken marriage—and I fell for it. I had not resisted the detours and distractions; instead I had willingly followed them, knowing the devastating consequences all the while. The devil had convinced me; I was too far gone to turn back. He knew he had me trapped in his snare once and for all. My life felt over, and my ministry was forever ruined.

Every dream I ever dreamed was gone.

Every gift and talent I had from God would never be used again.

Every message I spoke of God's love and mercy would be forgotten.

It was all over.

Or so he thought.

I walked around for a few years covered in my shame, buried in my guilt. Every ounce of insecurity and inferiority I had ever felt in my life was magnified by ten thousand. The fear of running into someone that knew what I had done, was overpowering at times. Looking my sweet dad in the eyes was heartbreaking. Trying to explain the unexplainable to my children was crushing. Satan thoroughly convinced me that I was a disgrace to God, to my family, and to myself.

But . . .

Out of my pain and out of my shame, rose the love of my Heavenly Father, greater and stronger than I had ever felt before. Quietly but persistently, day after day, I felt His love wash over me and bathe me in His forgiveness. The darkness that had blinded me eventually left, and I could see His light brighter and more beautiful than I ever had before. He had forgiven me the moment I had asked Him to years earlier, but now the time had come to start the process of forgiving myself. He had never stopped loving me through it all, and He still believed in me even while I no longer believed in myself. He picked me up, held me in His arms, and carried me for the next several years. He never let me go. When I felt the crippling shame and condemning eyes of others, He just held me tighter. His Words became my life source and sustained me during the darkest days I had ever experienced.

My salvation was no longer something I just took for granted— it was my everything.

Slowly, the real me, the one God knew was there all along, began emerging out from under the titles I deserved to wear: the failure, the loser, the quitter. I was finally able to stand to my feet on my own and receive my new titles: Finisher, Winner, Overcomer.

Through this extreme shame and suffering, I found out, I was not a quitter! I fought hard, and I won! He thought this was my final blow, but I'm still here, and I'm still standing! The devil is defeated in my life. He knocked me down, but he did not knock me out! I fell hard, but I got back up. He thought my faith in God was gone, but it came back stronger and deeper than ever before. He thought he would shut me up, and my voice would never be used again for God, but here I stand, sharing the love of Jesus, bolder and stronger than before! Today I confidently say, "I am a Savelle, and I am not a quitter," but more importantly, "I am a child of God, and I am a winner!" Quitting is no longer an option for me. I cannot be defeated, and I refuse to ever quit!

Arise from the depression
and prostration in which circumstances
have kept you—rise to a new life!
Shine (be radiant with the glory of the Lord),
for your light has come,
and the glory of the Lord has risen upon you!
Isaiah 60:1 (AMP)

Your story may be similar to mine or nothing like it, but wherever you've been or wherever you are, I wrote this book for you. You may want to quit and give up on everything this very moment.

You may feel like *What's the use?* But you can't quit!

I'm telling you to never quit and never give up on yourself.

Quitting is not an option for you anymore.

Compromise is not available either.

Just because your marriage is struggling, you can't throw in the towel. Divorce can't be the answer for every problem that arises in your marriage. You are not a quitter! You have to fight for your marriage, you have to fight the devil. He will try to get you to think:

Life would be easier without my husband.

I married the wrong guy.

I deserve better.

Don't entertain those thoughts.

You may have relapsed again with an old addiction, and you're thinking "I always go back." You can't give up now; your relapse doesn't mean you're forever a failure.

You're not a quitter!

He's out to destroy your life; don't fall prey to his schemes any longer.

Enough is enough!

The world says, "When things get hard, just quit," but you are not of this world; you belong to Jesus, and He gives you the power through the Holy Spirit to change your life. What the devil has meant for harm and destruction in your life, God can turn around. He gives beauty for ashes and joy instead of mourning (see Isaiah 61:3). No one has ever been so far down that God cannot lift them up. I've heard my dad say many times, "God is a master of making champions out of failures."

It's not how you start
It's how you finish that matters most.

The devil has done everything to try to keep you defeated in life. It's time to say, "No more!" Haven't you been knocked around long enough? Aren't you tired of taking two steps forward only to be pushed three steps back? Then get up, and start fighting back. Not with people but with the real enemy who is always trying to attack your life with chaos and confusion! First Peter 5:8 (AMP) says, "be vigilant *and* cautious at all times; for that enemy of yours, the devil, roams around like a lion roaring [in fierce hunger], seeking someone to seize upon *and* devour." See yourself picking up a whip and fighting back now. Determine to win this time! Don't let him devour your life anymore! He's beat you down long enough! No more cowering in the corner, letting him attack you through fear, addiction, and shame.

Arise from the ashes and show him who's boss!

You will be able to say to the devil, like Joseph did, "You planned something bad for me, but God produced something good from it" (Genesis 50:20 CEB).

You are a finisher and winner in Jesus!

I have to warn you, though, when you decide to come out from under the sin and despair you've been living in and begin standing up for God's divine purpose for your life, some people will not believe in you. In fact, some people may secretly hope you fail—just like you did last time. Sadly, some of those people might call themselves Christians. You will have to tighten your belt, grit your teeth, and push through the laughing, the gossip, the stares, and prove them wrong (I've had to do that!) Let them talk, and let them judge. You may have heard the saying before, "It's none of your business what others think of you." That's the mindset you're going to have to keep. Your ultimate goal in life now is to please God and not be concerned what others think. Remember, your past does not define you today. You are forgiven, and because of God's forgiveness, you have been made white as snow, and your slate has been wiped clean.

A few years ago, I began having a Bible study/book club in my home, stepping out in faith, even though fear tried it's best to overtake me. I had no idea if anyone would even show up or even care what I had to say. Thankfully, several precious friends came, and I encouraged them to invite others who might benefit from our little group. One friend informed me that she had invited this girl we both knew, but she had declined the invitation. In her words, she just couldn't "get past what I had done." I knew I had hurt many people, and I certainly don't make light of it, but at that moment, I had to decide, *Do I know that God still has a plan for my life by sharing His Word with others, or am I going to allow this woman to affect me and let all those feelings of inadequacy come crashing through?* I knew if I followed my feelings that I would quit. It stung for a moment, but I made the courageous decision to ignore her words and carry on. Remember, I'm not a quitter anymore. That first group was the rebirth of the ministry the Lord has given me today to bring hope to hurting women. What if I had quit?

We all want to be liked, but some people may not be on your side, cheering you on to victory. That's okay because God is! He believes in you when nobody else might. You can't control what people will think of you, but you can control how it affects you. I heard someone say, "My story is not perfect, but it's not finished." You have to push through the criticism and doubt from others; allow it to make you stronger, carrying on regardless of anyone's opinion of you.

Quitters quit when things get hard.

Quitters quit when people talk bad about them.

Quitters quit when nothing seems to be going right.

Quitters quit when temptations arise.

Quitters quit when they are afraid.

Winners never quit, *ever*!

Winners keep going when things get hard.

Winners keep going when people talk bad about them.

Winners keep going when nothing seems to be going right.

Winners keep going when temptations arise.

Winners keep going when they are afraid.

You are faithful, you are committed, you are determined . . . you are a winner!

66 GETTING KNOCKED DOWN IN LIFE IS A GIVEN. GETTING UP AND MOVING FORWARD IS A CHOICE. 99
ZIG ZIGLAR

The Pruning Process

Don't you love the idea of a fresh start?

A new beginning?

A second chance?

Being able to push delete and start over?

Thankfully, because of Jesus and His great love and grace for us, He gives us that opportunity as many times as we need it.

God made my life complete
when I placed all the pieces before him.
When I got my act together,
he gave me a fresh start.
Now I'm alert to God's ways;
I don't take God for granted.
Every day I review the ways he works;
I try not to miss a trick.
I feel put back together,
and I'm watching my step.
God rewrote the text of my life
when I opened the book of my heart to his eyes.
Psalm 18:20-24 (MSG)

I have one rose bush in my flower bed, planted by the previous owners of my home. Every year, beautiful bright pink roses bloom from it. Not too long ago, it dawned on me that summer had arrived, but I had not seen any roses this year. I realized that I had forgotten to prune it. I immediately went to hacking and trimming away on my one and only rose bush. Once finished, it stood looking scrawny and bald, but you know what? Not long after, I saw a tiny little flower popping through, and eventually it began to grow bigger and blossom. I know others will be popping out soon! This pruning reminds me of our lives and the process we have to go through to remove unprofitable things from our lives. Pruning your life (the act of getting rid of damaged, dead, and non-productive things) may hurt at first, and you probably will not enjoy exposing all the unproductive things, like getting rid of your old thought life, your bad habits, and your crippling insecurities.

You are now making the necessary changes to get on with your God-given purpose. But I can promise you that during the pruning process of life, the devil will bring every arsenal and tactic to make you quit and just accept the ugly parts of your life. He will attempt to use those old tricks that worked before:

An old boyfriend who was never right for you will show up out of the blue.

Someone will remind you of a bad choice you made.

Opportunities to go back to that old addiction will arise.

Trick him this time; don't fall for it anymore! It might hurt for a time, and it might be uncomfortable when certain things become exposed, but it's only temporary. If you can push through the tests and the uncomfortable way you feel when being pruned, you will begin to see positive changes gradually taking place. You will discover a more beautiful way to live that's waiting to blossom once you have the courage to remove the dead things. You may be like me and the rose bush; before pruning, I kept waiting to see a beautiful bloom from an unproductive bush. You might be waiting to see change in your life, hoping one day things will be different. But are you taking the necessary steps to rid your life of negative things?

Is it time to prune from your life someone who isn't good for you? Is it time to get rid of a destructive habit that you've been battling with for years? Is it time to stand up for yourself and stop being used?

Stay faithful on your quest of removing the unproductive things, and watch God transform the ugliness into something breathtakingly beautiful that others can admire. He will show you off and say, "Look at my one of a kind, prized rose. Isn't she beautiful!"

Make a commitment to remove things that need to be removed from your life.

Lay all the pieces before him, and let God show you the things that need to be removed from your life. When you ask the Holy Spirit to reveal those things to you, He will do it without harshness or condemnation. He will gently prune away the unprofitable, guiding you to the areas that need to be changed. That's what I had to do, even though it was uncomfortable at times, it was absolutely necessary for transformation in my life.

And we know that in all things God works for the good of
those who love him, who have been called
according to his purpose.
Romans 8:28 (NLT)

Hope and Expectancy

I love those two words: *hope* and *expectancy*. Expectancy is anticipating something coming in the future, and hope causes you to dream again. A life with no hope is a life just existing. Proverbs 13:12 (NKJV) says, "Hope deferred makes the heart sick." When something is deferred, it is put off or postponed. Hope causes you to live with purpose. Jeremiah 29:11 tells us that God has plans to give us hope and a future. He has good things in store for us.

Let all that I am wait quietly before God,
for my hope is in him.
Psalm 62:5 (NLT)

Hope is a flicker of light surrounded by the dark.

Hope carries on when everyone else has given up.

Hope stays the course.

Hope's counterpart is expectancy. When I think of the word expectancy, I can't help but think of the six times I've been expecting with my babies. It is one of the most amazing feelings in the world to have a life growing inside of you. From the minute you find out your expecting a baby, your thoughts are on that baby being born, constantly thinking on what is to come.

"Is it a boy? A girl?"

"How much will he weigh?"

"Will she look like me?"

An expectant mother prepares, plans, waits, and dreams for the moment of her precious baby's arrival. The anticipation can be overwhelming at times. She can hardly wait for that special day to approach, and then the due date arrives, and it's time. A new life and a new beginning has emerged! Finally holding that new bundle of love, you realize, from that moment on, things will never be the same!

When you finally get the junk (the shame, the guilt, the inferiority, the addictions, and the unforgiveness) out of your life through the pruning process and get on the path where God wants you, then you can begin to have hope through . . .

preparing,

planning,

waiting, and

dreaming.

Jeremiah also says, God wants to prosper you. The word *prosper* means "rich, wealthy, flourishing, living in abundance." Imagine your life right now prospering. Having money is great, but God's prosperity goes farther than just money. He can make you rich with peace of mind, a wealth of joy, and abundance in every area of your life. That's what total prosperity looks like, and you can expect that for your life when you completely yield to Him rather than your way.

You may be saying, "I've made a lot of changes in my life, but I don't see anything different." That's where having faith with expectancy kicks in. Faith is simply depending *entirely* on God and believing that He will do what He says He will do—if you don't give up and give in. You have to believe that He *will* give you a hope and a good future (a successful future)!

Expect your life to change for the better, and it will!

The key is staying focused on Jesus rather than on what could have happened, what hasn't happened, or what is happening to others. Stay focused with hope and expectancy on His plan for your life.

> *We have this hope as an anchor for the soul,*
> *sure and strong.*
> Hebrews 6:19 (NCV)

Having faith in God reminds me of planting a seed. You have

this tiny seed that comes in a package. On the front of the package is a beautiful picture of what you can expect that tiny seed to look like if you do all the necessary things required to grow your seed. You cannot just shove it in the ground and never go back and take care of it, yet expecting fruit from it. Faith is like that seed. You have a picture on the inside of you of what you want your life to be like, so you begin to water and fertilize your life with God's Word. You may not see anything happening yet, but you continue in the Truth and apply all the things we have talked about.

Guard your heart.

Change your thoughts.

Make godly choices.

Create good habits.

Forgive.

Walk in love.

Eventually you will see a breakthrough! A stem begins to come out from the dirt; it begins to grow and blossom. That's exactly like your life. If you will not give up and go back to your old way of doing things, you will eventually see your life growing and blossoming. It will take **diligence** and **discipline** on your part, but you can do this! See yourself beyond your present circumstances, and create the life you want. Always stay hopeful and expectant in God's faithfulness to fulfill His promises to you.

Your hard work will pay off, and you will be standing right

where God wanted you to be all along: in His perfect will for your life! Don't settle and just be satisfied with a mediocre life. I heard this phrase the other day, *God doesn't want us to just fly; He wants us to soar!* He doesn't want us just existing, He wants us living an exciting and fulfilling life.

Never give up hope. Always stay expectant.

Grace and Restoration

I, Jerriann Savelle, am the biggest example of a life that has been restored by the grace of God. I have already shared with you how horribly I have messed up and the damage I created with my actions. Yet, God still loves me so much. After humbly repenting, He has picked up the pieces, restored me, and continues to bless my life! That's how loving He is. That's what grace is—His unmerited favor. I don't deserve that kind of love, but He is such a good God and loving Father. There is nothing that compares to His grace.

> *My grace is enough; it's all you need. My strength comes into*
> *its own in your weakness.*
> 2 Corinthians 12:9 (MSG)

If you are a parent, then you have experienced your child messing up a time or two (or twenty or thirty). Your child may have lied to you, ignored what you said, or ran off to do something you told them not to. Their behavior obviously disappointed you, and you corrected them for their actions, but you moved on and continued loving them. No good parent keeps a long list of all the bad things their children have done and reminds them of it daily. Nor do you decide to kick them out of the family for it. Regardless of their wrong actions, you still love them and show mercy to your children by continually forgiving them when they mess up. My parents have demonstrated this kind of grace countless times in my life. God does the same with you. Some people have an image of God as a mean dictator up in Heaven ready to condemn every time you make a mistake. He's not like that at all. He may be disappointed in a bad decision, but He already knew you were going to mess up in the first place. He just continues right on loving you, forgiving you, and restoring you. He's a good Father. There may be consequences that have to be faced because of bad choices, but God is rich in love and never holds grudges. He wants to restore your life so you may experience a blessed life. He wants you to succeed, and He wants the very best for you.

Let your life reflect the goodness of God's restoration.

There were things He had predestined for me to do with my life, but I had gotten off course by doing my own thing. Now that I am back on the right course, I am once again doing those things meant for me to do. That's restoration God's way!

I may be older now, but I am right back where I am supposed to be. I don't want to be one of those people who others see and say, "Oh, she had amazing potential, but never lived up to it." I will finish the course He has set out for me.

Instead of shame and dishonor, you shall have a double portion of prosperity and everlasting joy!
Isaiah 61:7 (TLB)

What about you? Don't you want to finish the course that God planned for you? He can restore everything!

The dictionary defines *restoration* as a bringing back to a former position or condition. However, my dad explains in his book *From Devastation to Restoration* that God's definition of *restore* is even better! When God restores, it means to make better, improve, increase, and multiply! Isn't that awesome? He will make your life even better than before when you completely surrender your will and your ways to Him!

God can improve your life, increase your life, and multiply your life better than before all those bad things happened to you. He can restore your life in a greater way than before you made those poor choices and decisions.

With God's restoration, no remnant of your former life and your old self remains.

The new and improved you is alive, reinstated and reestablished His way.

It is never too late to get back on the road God wanted you on and find His restoration!

He can restore you from a divorce and bring the right spouse to your life.

He can restore a relationship that has been severed with a family member.

He can restore the years that have been stolen!

He can transform every failure and mistake into a victory! What you've been through is not too big for God to fix! He is a God so full of mercy and grace!

And I will restore to you the years . . .
Joel 2:25 (KJV)

Another amazing part of God's restoration in my life is the awesome girlfriends He has brought to me. To go from being someone who was actually fearful of relationships with other girls, I now have a beautiful array of friends—precious people who stand by my side, believe in me and like me . . . they really like me (sort of borrowed from Sally Fields Oscar speech)!

I've also been healed from the heavy blanket of depression that covered me for the majority of my life. How peaceful it is to no longer have sleepless nights filled with anxiety and turmoil. I have sweet sleep because my Daddy watches over me. I am 45 years old at the time of this writing, and I can *finally* say, "I AM FREE!"

I am healed! I am whole! I am restored! I am happy being me! Thank you, Jesus!

Are you ready to be restored? Are you ready to get on with your purpose and destiny? Are you tired of being defeated and reminded of your past? Let's pray now and be free for good from those things that have bound you for far too long? Are you ready?

Say this with me:

"Father in Jesus Name, I come to you now and bring everything that has been broken in my life. Everything that has kept me down and defeated. Once and for all, I remove this heaviness from my life, never to be picked up again. I am free from defeated living. I am forgiven. I forgive myself, and I forgive those who have hurt me. From this day forward, my life is restored, and I will begin walking in that restoration and freedom *today*. I know that you have an awesome plan for me! Thank you, Jesus, for your amazing grace! Amen."

I truly believe an important part of restoration is to let your life be a public display of God's goodness. By telling others your redemptive story, it shows how God was able to turn your trials and setbacks into your testimony. Don't hold back from letting others see His amazing grace in your life! God needs you; He needs your voice. In fact, He expects it from you. You have a story to tell, and only you can tell it in your way! Let your story be a blessing to help and inspire others to pursue healing and freedom too!

Let victory over your sins, your mistakes, and your weaknesses become your great story!

Be a reflection of His grace.

Share the Good News with others of what He has done.

Show the world what a person looks like who gets back up!

When you let your life represent God's restoration, it also continues to let the devil know loud and clear that he has been defeated in your life. God is so proud of you; He wants to show you off!

> 66 SETBACKS DON'T HAVE TO BE FINAL IN YOUR LIFE, THEY CAN BECOME STEPPING STONES TO A MAJOR VICTORY. 99
> *JERRY SAVELLE*

When I think of a life of restoration, I can't help but think of my friend Bobby. If anybody has been through hard times, Bobby has. He has experienced all kinds of personal tragedy, which developed into a drug and alcohol addiction. In sharing his story, he said he eventually went from "victim to volunteer" in his destructive behavior. It led to him spending time behind bars, 76 months in all. Through the help of AA, he was finally able to get his life together, surrendering completely to Christ. He says he has seen God's divine direction every step of the way in turning his life around. Bobby is now happily married with a beautiful family. He currently attends college, pursuing a counseling license to help others with chemical dependency. He has a good job, in a church he loves, and is passionate about telling others his story of restoration and healing. Piece by piece, his life has been restored. I'm so proud of him and so thankful to God for what he's done in Bobby's life.

I love stories like that!

Our God is a big God, and He can do big things in your life. He can return all that has been stolen from you—money, time, health! You name it; He can restore it!

Reclaim your life and all that has been taken from you!

It's rightfully yours!

Dream Again

There was a point in my life when I was just existing and going through the motions wondering if I would ever see my hidden dreams fulfilled. Fear, doubt, and life's ups and down had clouded my perception and my purpose. It wasn't until God did a complete overhaul of my life, through that pruning process we talked about, that I was able to dream for my life again. You're reading one of my dreams now—this book. The devil tried so many times to make me stop writing by trying to make me think, *Who would want to even read what you have to say . . . after what you did?*

I just continued to push through, saying to myself, *Somebody needs to hear what I have to say!* I may have quit writing for months at a time, but I refused to give up. It has always been my dream to share God's message of love and hope to others. Despite the setbacks, the trials, the mistakes, I am now fulfilling my dream.

What about you? Are you fulfilling your dreams, or have the circumstances of life jaded your dreams? Do they seem unattainable now?

Maybe you have let fear sneak back in. Perhaps you are just existing and going through the motions of life. Have stagnation and complacency crept in, trying to pressure you into aborting those dreams?

> **IF YOU DON'T DREAM, YOU MIGHT AS WELL BE DEAD.**
> *GEORGE FOREMAN*

The devil wants to keep you so bogged down with past failures and defeats that you never attempt to dream big again. He also brings daily diversions (money issues, marriage problems, etc.) to get you distracted from pursuing your dreams. But, if you let Him, God can unfold your dreams again. From this point on, you can no longer have the mindset of "what could have been." Instead, you should think, dream, and pursue "what can be!"

It's time to dream again and dream big! Dig up those dreams

that have been hidden in your heart. They still exist. You might have to look deeply, but they have never left you. They were placed there by God; your life's quest, your self-worth, and your very reason for living are found in discovering your God given purpose. Dust those big dreams off, and dare to believe that God can bring them to pass.

Become courageous and unstoppable in your pursuit!

Don't wait for tomorrow or for next week or for a new year, start today! In his book, *Your Road To Recovery,* Oral Roberts said, "Nobody else can dream your dreams."

Set your sights higher than where you are today!

Live life with vision and purpose. Proverbs 29:18 says, "Where there is no vision, the people perish." It's easy to just exist like many people do, but just existing in life will always keep you unfulfilled. If you are existing only to continue your mediocre existence, what is the point? There is more to life than just maintaining. Quite honestly, you are miserable with no purpose. Imagine the person you want to be and the life you want to live, and pursue after it passionately. You can be anything you set your mind to.

Dream of a better marriage?

Dream of going back to school?

Dream of a new job?

Dream of living securely?

Then do something everyday to accomplish those dreams, bringing them into fruition. Dreaming big pulls you out of your comfort zones.

Find out how much it will cost to get started. Look up when classes begin, and get enrolled. Go sign up at the gym. Sit down and start writing chapter one.

Whatever your dream of accomplishment in life is, take the steps, and go for it!

I was talking to someone the other day who wants more out of life then the way he is currently living, but is unwilling to do what it takes to make it a reality because there's work involved. Yes, going after success is hard work, but hard work produces good things.

It takes striving, pushing, and reaching with determination to have the life God has promised.

Second Timothy 6:12 tells us to "Fight the good fight of faith." In the Easy-to-Read translation is goes on to say, "We have to fight to keep our faith. Try as hard as you can to win that fight. Take hold of eternal life. It is the life you were chosen to have when you confessed your faith in Jesus."

This is not the time to be sitting on the couch any longer, feeling sorry for yourself, wondering when life is going to get better. Change your situation now! It requires diligence and discipline, but there is great reward in finishing your course.

So I run straight to the goal with purpose in every step. I fight to win. I'm not just shadow-boxing or playing around. Like an athlete I punish my body, treating it roughly, training it to do what it should, not what it wants to.

1 Corinthians 9:26-27 (TLB)

Just like the scripture says, you must have purpose in every step, and you must fight to win! Lace up those shoes and begin walking with purpose! You only have one life to live, so live it with meaning.

Don't sit on the sidelines in the game of life, watching other people fulfill their dreams. Get in there, and go for it!

I know this girl from high school, named Lisa. We reconnected several years ago online. She has raised her three beautiful children and now has an empty nest. She decided to pursue her passion of photography. I've watched her strive and go after her dream. She's truly amazing at her work and is constantly booked with sessions because of her talent with the lens. I love the name of her company, Camralynz, the beginning of each of her children's names. It all began with a dream she had to do something she loved, while bringing joy to others through her craft.

God-given dreams always involve others.

God-given dreams will never be selfish in motivation—they will never be all about you. They will always have a positive impact on others and be a blessing in some way. Getting outside of yourself and helping others is the most fulfilling way to live. It feels so good to get to a place in life when you no longer focus on yourself, but instead are intent on helping others.

Accomplishing the dreams God has put inside of you becomes your very reason for living—your destiny and purpose. I loved what I heard Lisa Bevere say one time, "You are an answer, not a problem! There is a problem out there, and you are the answer!" That's doing the works of Jesus by helping and being a blessing to someone else. That is your purpose.

I have another friend Courtney, who I've known since the day she was born. She recently began an outreach for children around the world. She's reached out to Uganda, India, and she's making plans for more outreaches in other countries. Her goal is to empower kids through sports, dance, and music, while sharing the love of God. Reaction Tour supplies children with sports equipment, uniforms, and Bibles. It all began with a God-given thought, and that thought became a God-given dream. She is living in her dream. She had to make the choice to go for it, and she did!

Find your passion again. Stir the embers of those dreams flickering inside, and go for it! Don't ever give up on yourself regardless of what the devil has thrown your way. Every dream comes with tests and challenges.

Don't you see: everything you've ever been through in your life comes down to this moment right now? Will you let your past continue to dictate your life, or will you let God uncover your dreams and destiny? Trust in Him; He can revive what He placed down inside of you, but you must believe in yourself again! You've got what it takes to finish your race and win!

God has never given up on you. "Being confident of this, that he who <u>began</u> a good work in you <u>will</u> carry it on to completion until the day of Christ Jesus" (Philippians 1:6 NIV). He still has a plan and purpose specifically for your life, but only you can see it through to a flourishing finish.

For those of you who are stay-at-home moms, I know you still have dreams too. Yes, you love your children and enjoy taking care of your family; that is all part of God's plan for your life, but often times, your dreams can get lost in the mundane routine chores of life—those dreams you specifically have for yourself as an individual. You may have wondered, "There has to be more to life than making lunches, helping with homework, and carpooling." Believe me, I've been there and know that feeling, but God has not forgotten.

There *is* more for you.

He has seen your silent tears, and He knows the secret dreams and desires of your heart in the midst of doing your daily chores. Maybe it's a new business venture, record an album, getting involved with an outreach. In your quiet time, rediscover those dreams, goals, and passions and get started on whatever it is you want to be doing, along side being a wife or mother. Get out of your comfort zone, stretch yourself, rise higher in your thinking and soar to great places!

Dream . . . Desire . . . Discover . . . then Do!

Let the light that's on the inside of you come out shining. Be the light in a dark world. Make a difference in your family, your workplace, and your community.

There's no one else who can shine quite like you. Your shine is unique, so go and shine brightly!

You are the world's light—
a city on a hill, glowing in the night for all to see.
Don't hide your light! Let it shine for all.
Matthew 5:14-15 (TLB)

I sense you stirring now! You want this, don't you?! Everything you were created to be is found in God's plan for your life. He has already put everything in you to fulfill your purpose. Ephesians 1:11 says, "It's in Christ we find out who we are and what we're living for" (MSG). You were made for greatness!

Don't hold back any longer.

Reach for more in your life.

Get up and step out.

Procrastination is now a thing of the past.

Rise above the fear.

Break through the barriers.

Push through the limitations you have had.

Be confident in your uniqueness! The world is waiting for your gifts. Remember there is only one you, and you were created on purpose **with a purpose**! Be happy being you! Love yourself and don't let anything or anyone hold you back ever again! Embrace this moment of time you were given and go for it! You are a winner; now get to winning!

It is amazing, even fantastic,

how our God permeates every facet of our lives

and works His purposes

despite our human faults and failures.

He transforms our weaknesses

into channels of strength.

Our emptiness becomes

a vessel of His fullness,

our spiritual poverty

the basis for His eternal grace.

Our errors and mistakes

are stepping-stones for success.

Our defeats are only incidents

on the road to victory.

Psalm 113 (Psalms now)

Jerriann Savelle is the oldest daughter of well-known world evangelist, Jerry Savelle (and mom, Carolyn). She was raised a preacher's kid in a godly, faith-filled home. Like so many others though, she chose the wrong paths and made bad decisions for many years of her life. Finally, she put her full reliance in Jesus.

In her down to earth and transparent way, Jerriann is called to help others by sharing her story of hope, healing and freedom from low self-esteem, damaged emotions, and broken relationships. She desires to travel the world with the message of God's redeeming grace and mercy. Jerriann is an author, speaker and mother to six beautiful children in Granbury, Texas.

For more information about Jerriann and additional ministry resources:

Jerriann Ministries
P.O. Box 1354
Granbury, TX 76048

jerriannministries@gmail.com

jerriann.org

Follow Jerriann on facebook/instragram/twitter: @jerriannsn